D1262616

From a World Apart

A Little Girl in the Concentration Camps

Francine Christophe

Translated by Christine Burls

With an introduction by Nathan Bracher

University of Nebraska Press

Lincoln and London

Publication of this book
was assisted by a grant
from the National
Endowment for the Arts.

To Mimi,
the marketstall keeper,

Monsieur and
Madame Baux,
our concierges,

Madame Delay,
the garage owner,

Madame Périn,
my headmistress,

Monsieur Rouger,
a neighbor,

Clo Avy-Prégniard,
an artist,

Charles Streiff,
*a colonel in the
gendarmerie,*

And to all those
who helped us,
or even simply
pitied us

Contents

Introduction

Francine's Photos:

Windows on Humanity

NATHAN BRACHER

As the author herself has pointed out, what follows is
neither a sweeping narrative of a world at war – of which
there are many excellent examples, since events often did
indeed take on epic dimensions – nor even a documen-
tary of the Holocaust. We find instead a rather unassum-
ing, fragmentary collection of what she has aptly termed
"photos." And yet these snapshots of ordinary people
striving to fulfill the most mundane human needs in these
most extraordinary circumstances are windows that open
to a world far removed from our own historical time, as
well as from our day to day life. Indeed, warns Francine, "I
am no longer of your world, I am from a world apart . . .
from the world of the camps. . . ." And although daily
news reports in the last decade of the twentieth century
have been a stark reminder that ethnic conflict and even
genocide continue even fifty years after the cannons of
World War II have been silenced, we by and large keep
these events in the margins of our minds, since most of us
find it difficult to connect them with our own experience.
It is precisely here that Francine's modest testimony
proves invaluable: in recollecting her experiences of the
camps and assembling them into this "photo" album,
Francine has opened a series of windows that allow us
to go back and forth between the past and the present,
our "normal" world and the world of the camps.

Francine has dedicated her book not to any renowned political leader or military hero but to friends, neighbors, and acquaintances from all walks of life. Such are the people we find depicted throughout the text, and such were those who found themselves caught up in the maelstrom of events that swept over Europe during World War II. Perhaps some of Francine's most unsettling snapshots are those of the children: as captured in Francine's "photos," their empty, bewildered eyes and listless gazes peer through the decades now separating us from that era, and summon our minds and our conscience.

How was it possible for these children, who Francine describes being herded through Drancy to be arrested, snatched away from their parents (as is evident from the nail marks left by mothers and fathers desperately clinging to them), detained behind barbed wire in concentration camps in France, thrown into sealed boxcars for a journey (similar to the one that Francine and her mother had to endure between Poitiers and Drancy) that could last several days in searing heat or in frigid cold, and finally led to Auschwitz (which was the final destination for the vast majority of Jews deported from the Drancy camp in the northern suburb of Paris)? And, given France's long heritage of humanism and democratic ideals, how could such things have occurred with, in many instances, the active cooperation of French police, administrators, and government officials?

The answers to these questions are neither short nor simple. In France, as in other European countries, not only scholars and historians but also many public institutions are still, along with the general public, debating the many issues connected with these questions and struggling to come to terms with a painful past. And perhaps it is precisely because the necessity of setting the record straight has in recent years coincided with the urgency of stopping genocides in Kosovo, Bosnia, and Rwanda that public attention on both sides of the Atlantic has been focused even more acutely on the plight of the Jews, as evidenced not only by the crimes-against-humanity trials of Paul Touvier and Maurice Papon, but also, and perhaps more importantly, by the unceasing stream of books, articles, films, and television programs devoted to World War II and the plight of the Jews in France.

I shall not, in the context of this preface, presume to set the record straight on all these complex issues. I would, however, like to suggest a framework for approaching the Occupation and the Holocaust in France, one that has proven to be useful for me as someone twice removed from the events. I say twice removed, because, as I suspect will be the case for many readers of Francine's text, I am a baby boomer born almost a decade after the second World War, and because I am an American, whose country had an experience of the war that was quite different from that of France.

For the most part, we Americans like to hark back to the World War II years as a time of military triumph, economic strength, and great national unity. For France, however, World War II was to bring a crushing defeat and virtual civil war, as the German Occupation divided the country into several zones, confiscated an enormous portion of industrial and agricultural production, and ultimately pitted the Resistance and De Gaulle's Free France against the Collaborators and Vichy. And while for Americans, World War II was an era of national consensus around the ideals of patriotism and democracy – or at least we like to think of it as such – it was for France a time of moral and political confusion. For it was under the authority of a widely revered and highly respected military hero from World War I, Marshal Philippe Pétain, that the Vichy government enacted a series of measures that gradually excluded Jews from social and economic life and complied with German demands for quotas of Jews to be "deported to the East," to use the language of the time.

The first part of Francine's account attests to the many hardships of the German Occupation that Francine and her mother endured along with their fellow French citizens: shortages of basic commodities, rationing, waiting in line, hunger, disappearances of friends and loved ones, and fear. Like thousands of other French school children, Francine sings "Maréchal, nous voilà" in honor of Pétain and even wins the "Marshal Pétain Prize" as the best pupil among the children of prisoners of war. And yet for all his grandfatherly, distinguished old gentleman appearance, the renowned military leader from World War I who presented himself as a sort of patriotic savior wishing only to preserve and rebuild France after the debacle of May and June 1940, based his regime on scapegoating and exclusions. The divisive, vindictive nature of his Vichy regime is particularly evident in the treatment reserved for Jews.

For once in power, Pétain immediately set out on a series of drastic, reactionary reforms known, strangely enough, as the "National Revolution": "Liberté, Égalité, Fraternité," the watchwords of democratic institutions, were replaced by "Travail, Famille, Patrie" ("Work, Family, Country"), for Pétain was intent on returning to a social and political order based on "natural" hierarchies, religion, and tradition. Pétain's autocratic, sectarian approach was based on the widely held (and deeply flawed) perception of France's crushing defeat by Germany as a sanction, that is, as history's judgment on the moral and political decadence of the Third Republic. And since one of the sources of this decadence was allegedly the pervading presence of "foreign" and "anti-French" elements in society and culture, Jews became scapegoats for the defeat and were often presented in the press and on the radio as a group that needed to be purged from French society. Such rhetoric was all too often translated into action. Only a week after France's democratic constitution had been scuttled on 10 July 1940 to create Pétain's authoritarian Vichy regime, Jews were excluded from all government jobs. And just a few weeks later, strict quotas would limit the number of Jews practicing law and medicine to a tiny fraction. Other measures soon stripped 7,000 naturalized Jews and 115,000 Algerian Jews of their citizenship, authorized virulent anti-Semitic attacks in the press, and authorized prefects to place all foreign Jews in internment camps or in forced labor units. As the war progressed, restrictions became more and more severe as Jews were banned from virtually all public places: neither parks, nor theaters, nor cafés, nor museums, nor libraries, nor restaurants were open to them. Moreover, they were required to shop only during certain designated hours, and, upon the insistence of the Germans, they were forced to wear the yellow Star of David prominently displayed on their clothing.

These policies imposed great hardships upon Jews, driving them out of the social and economic mainstream and setting them apart as objects of exclusion and scorn. Many French Jews lost their jobs and their businesses, while foreign Jews were often either locked up in camps or forced into a precarious clandestine existence. But the most damaging actions were yet to come. At the instigation of the Germans, France used its own administrative apparatus and its own police to identify, locate, and arrest tens of thousands of Jews, detain them in squalid camps, and then turn them over to the Germans for deportation.

It is perhaps useful at this juncture to trace rapidly the contours of the Holocaust as it affected France. Out of some 330,000 Jews living in France at the outset of the war, over 76,000 fell victim to genocide. We must always remember, however, that it was not the French but the Germans who demanded quotas of Jews for deportation, issued orders for deportation, and ran the killing centers in Eastern Europe. While Vichy set in place a whole series of anti-Jewish laws and policies, it never had the intention of exterminating Jews, nor did it take the initiative of the Final Solution. There were no death camps on French soil. Nevertheless, regardless of any knowledge or ignorance of the ultimate destination of the deportees, the political and administrative machinery of the Vichy government actively participated in the "Final Solution."

This is the painful legacy that France has been coming to terms with for the last twenty-five years. But we must remember that, while Vichy must bear a heavy responsibility for most of the 76,000 Jews from France who lost their lives, most of the 250,000 Jews who survived (and France had the highest survival rate of any country occupied by the Nazis) can be grateful to the French people who hid, fed, or simply refused to denounce them. Even on the minimal level of benign indifference, it was essential.

Equally essential, for those such as Francine and her mother who did not manage to escape arrest, detention, and deportation, were their courageous efforts not only to survive, but also to hold on to what human dignity they could in these extreme circumstances and even to reach out and help others. For in the face of unspeakable suffering and terror, Francine and her mother, along with others, organize classes, celebrate birthdays and national holidays, make toys and decorations, and put on talent shows. Francine's mother in particular devotes herself to caring for others and relieving their suffering to the extent possible.

In the context of camps, these brave efforts are of special significance and belie two common myths: that Jews passively allowed themselves to be killed and that the camps succeeded in dehumanizing the captives within. For as Tzvetan Todorov points out, the camps were specifically designed to deprive people of their humanity.[1] As graphically related in Francine's text, detainees were deprived of all human privacy and modesty, since they were forced to undress and expose themselves; they were physically degraded by severe malnutrition and a lack of the most basic hygiene that sometimes made them live in their own excretions; they were totally depersonalized, since they were designated by numbers, and constantly referred to not by name but by insults and racial slurs.

And yet they refused. They refused to give up hope, and in the case of Francine and her mother, the fight against despair and degradation finally enabled them to survive. As Susan Zucotti has remarked, simply surviving in such extreme circumstances required moral and physical resistance to all the forces aimed at extermination.[2] Francine's moving testimonial thus belies the persistent myth of Jews letting themselves be "passively led like lambs to be slaughtered." Her "photo album" similarly contradicts the notion that the camps successfully stripped detainees of the "artifices" of human dignity and morality. For in the face of the systematic degradation aimed at destroying any sense of human dignity and spontaneity, Francine, her mother, and many others depicted resisted by showing compassion and creativity.

If there are any "lessons" to be learned from her harrowing account, surely we must retain first and foremost a great lesson about humanity. For while the hallucinatory scenes from the camps indeed come from "another world," they involve, as Tzvetan Todorov has again reminded us, the one and same humanity as our own. As sadly evidenced not only by the legacy of World War II, but also by the unsettling instances of "ethnic cleansing" and genocide that have marked the end of the twentieth century, "ordinary" human beings including the French and the Germans and all other nationalities, are capable of inflicting the most horrific suffering on their fellow human beings, particularly when the latter have been singled out as belonging to some supposedly inferior or undesirable race, ethnicity, or social group. But it is also such "ordinary" people, and not great military heroes or other larger-than-life historical figures, who, even though subjected to a regime of terror and degradation, testify to the universal human virtues of dignity, care, and creativity. Even Francine's criticisms of her shortfalls, in instances when the pangs of hunger and cold seem to overcome what remains of compassion and wit within her, are a tribute to her humanity: by probing the depths of her own self, she contributes not only to our knowledge of this particular time in history, but also to our common human identity. Surely we would do well to look long and hard and to emulate her example of courage, compassion, and lucidity.

NOTES

1. Tzvetan Todorov, *Face à l'extrême* (Paris: Éditions du Seuil, 1994), pp. 190–96.
2. Susan Zucotti, *The Holocaust, the French, and the Jews* (New York: Basic Books, 1993; reprint, Lincoln: University of Nebraska Press, 1999), p. 277.

From a World
Apart

T his is not a full account, but a series of snap-shots. Many have been lost in my childhood memory, some have yellowed with age; I have kept only the clear images.

What follows is totally without literary pretension. From the age of twelve, I noted down my memories as they emerged from the spiritual desert into which suffering had plunged me, thinking even then that I should bear witness.

This little book was therefore inside my head.

It took me only a few weeks to compose it in 1967, bringing together my ideas and notes.

I was a privileged little girl, because my father had been taken prisoner. And curious as it seems, that is what saved my life.

It all begins in Deauville, where Granny has rented a villa for the whole family: Uncle Daniel, Aunt Suzanne, their two daughters, Father, Mother, and myself.

Deauville in August '39, the sea and sand, the stroll from the town to the beach in long white bath robes, the children's club beach balls, taller than ourselves, onto which we are hoisted to be photographed.

And one day, when we come home, the radio is blaring in the house. Father and Mother go up to their room, very pale: Father comes back down wearing a suit and tie.

Kisses, smothering kisses, arms wrapped tightly, hearts bursting. The station, the train. And the radio that blares on about pink and blue forms.

I am six years old.

Later, Granny and Uncle Charles (he is Granny's second husband and we don't call him Grandpa) rent an apartment in Cimiez, above Nice. I go to school there and instantly pick up the lilting accent of the South.

Father obtains his first leave. Mother goes to pick him up at the station, and the way they look at each other fills me with contentment.

We go for a walk on the Promenade des Anglais. Mother is very beautiful, Father is magnificent with his double braided officer's cap, and I feel rather splendid myself with my grey coat from Mirkey, rue Saint Honoré, the shop founded by my grandmother.

Like the soldiers, I'm wearing a little army cap, the same grey as my coat.

Back to Paris.

People are saying it's a "funny kind of war"[1] (*une drôle de guerre*), and indeed it is funny to go to school with a satchel in one hand and a gas mask in the other.

We live with Grandmother, on the rue Saint Honoré. The primary school on the rue de la Ville l'Evêque is next to an old house with a deep cellar, where we rehearse air raid drills. One of my school friends has a prettier mask than mine, funnier too, with a little capsule you can take off. Mine ends in a tube. I look like a funny elephant.

The way Mother helps me prepare my things every evening is funny too, woollen underwear on top of the pile (we mustn't catch cold in the cellars!).

Ah! If only Father were here too, how much fun the war would be.

June 1940. I'm six and a half. We are at La Baule, for a new kind of holiday, which Mother calls an "exodus."

She and I take a room with some local people; Aunt Suzanne and the girls come too.

People are going crazy everywhere. One day, the lines for the shops stretch all the way down the street and everything on the shelves disappears.

We have to cross the Loire, say the grown-ups. "We'll leave tomorrow with Aunt Suzanne, who has a car."
    And bang! The next day I have German measles . . . it lasts forty-eight hours, but it's already too late. Forty-eight hours later, I watch a stream of roaring motorbikes go by, ridden by very young, very handsome (the invasion troops had been carefully chosen for their good looks), very well dressed (all in green) . . . and very well armed, soldiers.

On the radio, we hear an appeal from a French general saying that one day we will win the war. Few people hear this appeal, but our landlady's son, a saddler, is leaving immediately to join this general, so he says.

A few days later, everyone has to take their radios along to the police station.

We have to return to Paris. With difficulty, we find two places in a train full of refugees from the North, now returning home because the invasion troops are every-where.

For the journey, Mother puts an apron on me, and as I complain about it, says:
"These people have lost everything, darling, we mustn't make them feel worse by parading such a pretty dress."

So I keep my apron on.

Father was fighting in Amiens during the bombing of the town. Apparently the commanding officers left, and Father brings the remainder of his men back to the Loire alone. This is called the Amiens retreat.

From Clisson, he sends us a photo showing his beard and hollow cheeks.
Many officers have been grouped together there, and the high command makes them give their word of honor as French officers that they will not desert.

They all give their word . . . and are all taken prisoner.

The Germans send them to Laval.

We set off there. We stay in a family boarding house and eat at a restaurant.

One lunchtime, a German soldier calls me over and offers me a sweet. "She never eats sweets!" cries Mother . . . "As you wish, my dear." And he laughs.

When he leaves, the waitress explains that he had been

a barber in the neighboring street for the past five years and has just revealed his nationality and spying activities.

He knows everyone and everyone is afraid of him.

As for Father, he is staying in the Grand Séminaire at Laval. On our first visit there, he explains that around 6,000 officers occupy a seminary meant for 150, that they sleep anywhere and everywhere, in the corridors, the toilets, the kitchens, and . . . that they eat out of the chamber pots, buckets, and so on belonging to the nuns who did the cooking for the young priests. I think it's a bit dirty.

18 August 1940. I am seven.

Mother buys a huge cake and we leave for the Seminary.
At the entrance, the sentry on duty goes through all the
parcels and shakes the cake box violently.

"The imbecile!" cries Mother. Then she blanches and
adds, "No, no, he can't have understood!" Neither did I.

We rejoin Father and his companions, who look worried
when she tells them what she said.

We eat my cake, crushed, broken, but delicious all the
same. Father and Mother kiss. It's hot, the grass is limp.
What a wonderful seventh birthday.

Two days later, at visiting time, a mass of green-clad,
armed soldiers bar the entrance.

Mother obtains permission to embrace Father. And,
under the surveillance of the sentinels, Father holds us
very close.

We leave Laval, and a friend who saw it himself confirms the prisoners' departure.

I don't understand what a camp is, I have no idea where Germany is, but now I understand what a war is.

Once again, we return to our apartment in Paris, and I set off for my school in the rue Jouffroy.

From time to time, Father sends a kind of long, unsealed folding letter, with lots of sentences crossed out in red and notes in the margin. Censorship, apparently.

A cold winter, with lots of deep snow. Mother explains that she has so little money to feed me that she prefers to send me to the canteen, where she hopes I'll eat better.

Winter 1940–41.

Everyone who owns arms of any sort must take them to the police. We have two hunting rifles, a fencing foil (Father fences), and even a "Joan of Arc sword," which an actress on tour had left him as a souvenir when he was a student. With the help of the concierge, Monsieur Baux, we throw everything into the Seine, except for the fencing foil and the sword, which Mother takes to the police station in contempt.

Many other people do the same.

All the Jewish shopkeepers must display a sign saying JEW in their window, in big letters. I don't really understand what it means and slip back into the childish habit of endlessly asking why.

But, by some unanimous decision, as well as the obligatory JEW, in every window flourish the family's medals and military achievements.

In the window of her shop "Francine Pary" (which she founded and named after her granddaughter), Grandmother places all the family's medals and a notice saying that Uncle Maurice fought in the Dardanelles, that Uncle George was gassed etc., etc.

Opposite, in the jeweler E . . .'s window, I have never seen so many medals rewarding the owner's acts of courage in the First World War.

Seeing this, the police have everything removed, even the yellow JEW signs.

At Christmas, I have just a branch of fir tree, because there's a war on.

And in my shoe, I find a bar of chocolate marked "for Father," which I will put in the next parcel. There is also a letter from Father.

What a splendid Christmas.

All through the spring and summer, I play hopscotch on the pavement with the postman's daughter.

In the evening, Mother goes down to the concierge's to listen to the radio in secret.

In one of his letters, Father must have described something that didn't please the censors. In the margin, opposite the crossed out passage, there's a note: "This is too much."

December 1941. They come to arrest Father. The concierges have difficulty explaining that Father isn't here, that he's a prisoner in Germany.

I find Mother strange, as if she were afraid.

In the evenings, with our neighbor whose husband is also a prisoner, she goes to the closest fruit and vegetable stall in the rue de Lévis to pick up wilted and discarded vegetables and then she joins the line . . .

Uncle Alfred, Granny's brother, sometimes takes us out to a restaurant. Mother wears a beautiful lace hat in his honor, and says, as she puts it on: "Just imagine what people must think when they see me with my hat and Alfred."

Then Uncle Alfred suddenly leaves Paris for the provinces.

From time to time, we receive a parcel of vegetables from him.

We no longer talk openly about Uncle Alfred.[2]

The lines in front of the food shops are getting longer, only to obtain, after several hours wait, a few potatoes or a little oil.

Mother prepares a delicious chestnut cake with . . . broad beans!

A story is going round:

Two very genteel ladies are talking about cooking.
    "Oh! My dear, I make an amazing chocolate cake."
    "My dear friend, do give me the recipe . . ."
    "Well, I don't use any chocolate, flour, eggs, sugar, or butter . . ."
    "And is it good?"
    "No!"

Mother says that we are Jews and because of that, we are not allowed out after eight o'clock.

Returning from Maud's, the wife of a prison comrade of Father's, on Boulevard Exelmans, we find that the Auteuil train station has been closed early. We have to take the metro. It's risky at that time of night. I'm sweating with fear and we get back to the house five minutes late, our hearts pounding, for now they arrest people for the slightest misdemeanor.

Why, Mother?

I can sing *"Maréchal nous voilà"* ("Marshall, here we are") as well as anyone.

Even Georges Lévy,[3] a World War I veteran, thinks Pétain[4] is helping us and many other Jews do too.

We are no longer allowed to travel.

We are no longer allowed to work.

We are only allowed to do our shopping during closing hours. A few shopkeepers who know us well prepare parcels for us, but it is dangerous.

Mother lines up for half the day at the police headquarters to register us, by order of the *Kommandatur*.

Then, at the local police station, they stamp our identity cards with the word JEW in big red letters.

As some people rub it out, they perforate the word JEW with little holes.

Someone said that when your name is CHRISTOPHE, you don't need to declare yourself as a Jew, but Mother replies that she has always obeyed the law.

And anyway, just because we're declared, it doesn't mean that they'll do us any harm.

By the way, Mother, what does it mean to be Jewish? Every evening you make me say your special prayer:

"Dear God, protect my family and my friends, and make me a better person so that I do good to those around me."

Does that have anything to do with it?

Father's cousin, Physician-General Gustave Worms,[5] director of the Val-de-Grâce hospital, is removed from his post because he is Jewish. He takes refuge in Saint-Aignan, but before they have time to arrest him, he dies of grief.

I'm eight and a half. I am doing well at school. One month top of the class, the next, second.

One Sunday, Mother sews yellow stars marked JEW in black gothic letters onto our clothes.

We had to wait a long time to obtain them, giving up our precious textile rations (there will be that much less to clothe ourselves) and, I believe, pay for them.

We go out for lunch at Grandmother's.

Yes, Mother is young, pretty, and refined looking. Yes, I am eight years old, with golden ringlets that I curl using my hoop baton.

Yes, everyone looks at us, and Mother tells me I've always stood up very straight and that now I should do so even more.

We go for a walk on rue Saint Honoré with Grandmother, and a lady we know crosses the road to shake our hands and say that the star looks very fine on black.

Last week, I asked my best friend at school if she would still play with me, because I am no longer like her, and the proof will be written on my chest.

She didn't really understand. And what about me?

And on Monday morning, I leave for school with my star covering nearly my whole left side.

When I go into the playground, all the little girls look at me. The headmistress kisses me.

I stand up very straight, Mother said so. And since I have to be Jewish, I'll do it with a smile, without flinching.

In the metro, the ticket collector asks us timidly to go to the last carriage, the only one we are allowed to use.

Under the school porch, two classmates pinched me. Their parents had told them that I deserved no better.

But when I came out of school, Mimi, the lady from the fruit and vegetable stall on Place Tocqueville, kissed me as a German officer was going by!

Posters appear on the walls, inviting those looking for work to go along to designated offices for an undemanding and well paid job.

An elderly lady from our *quartier* takes Mother by the sleeve:

"You know, Madame Christophe, I went along there, because I'm in need of work. Ah! But I'm not one of them! Do you know what they wanted me to do? To sit behind closed shutters in a ground floor apartment, so I could listen to conversations and report them to the police. And also inform on any Jews who had not declared themselves. No, it wasn't demanding. I'd rather not eat!"

Our stars have to be sewn on and not pinned, subject to verification.

A few people have been arrested because they attach theirs with snap fasteners.

A young girl is imprisoned because she has sewn lace around her star.

A gentleman who was telling his child to put his handkerchief in his pocket (*poche*) has just been taken away by a German soldier who thought he had heard the word "Boche." An insult to the occupying forces.

Those who are arrested are never seen again.

All public places are strictly forbidden to us: museums, theaters, cinemas, parks, cafés.

I look enviously at the Parc Monceau. Through the bars, I can see my friends.

I try to get into the Square des Batignolles, to join my friend, but because of the star on my chest, I'm sent back out. So I stand there stupidly, shifting from one foot to the other, admiring the trees and the flowers from a distance, trying to hear what the other children are shouting as they play.

I don't mind wearing the star, but let me be with my friends. For heaven's sake, I don't smell bad!

Mother continues to listen to the English radio at the concierges' apartment. At the slightest sound, she runs out through the back door, which opens directly onto the stairs.

People are being arrested everywhere. Round-ups in the metro, at the doors of the synagogues (which we do not attend, because our family is not religious), at the school gates, where children with stars are taken away with no warning to their parents.

The metro stations and streets fill with enormous posters showing us with pointed chins, evil eyes, thick lips, hooked noses, clawed hands, heads covered with rags.

At least one thing makes us laugh: the only member of the family who looks like these posters is Uncle Charles, Granny's second husband, and he is Aryan and Catholic.

Everywhere, Jewish apartments are emptied. One afternoon, on rue Cardinet, we see our friends the Lévy de Souza's furniture being taken away.

Mimi, the fruit and vegetable lady, offers us the garage where she parks her cart. My dearest Naine, our ex-maid, her apartment. Madame Delay, the garage-owner, her attic, where in the middle of the night we transport Father's big horse picture and leather armchair, carried by two taxi drivers whose cars she houses.

Maud Narçon, whose father is a prisoner with mine, rents a room in his name in our building, and Madame Baux, the concierge, lends us one of hers.

Thus, little by little, a part of Father's library is hidden away, as well as some furniture and a few family heirlooms.

Mother is afraid. I am afraid. Everywhere, all the time, people with stars disappear and never return.

Father is also afraid, for from his camp, he hears of the arrests.

In the private code that he and Mother invented in 1940, he begs us to get to the Unoccupied Zone and to join his brother Daniel, Suzanne, and the girls.

I'm frightened, Mother. Last year, I was seven years old. This year, I'm eight, and so many years separate these two ages.

I have learnt that I am Jewish, that I am a monster, and that I must hide myself.

I'm frightened all the time.

And when I receive the Maréchal Pétain Prisoner of War's Children's Award for brightest pupil and the prize is entitled "The Saints' Lives," I laugh very loudly, because I'm frightened to death.

Father is sent to a prison camp in Nuremberg, then to Edelbach in Austria.

The World War I veterans are set free. So Monsieur Co-quard, from the third floor, my friend Geneviève's father, comes back to France.

The Jewish veterans are set free too. But when they arrive in Paris, they are made to take off their uniforms. So, as they are no longer soldiers, the Geneva Convention no longer protects them . . .

And, wham! they arrest them as Jews and send them back to Germany as deportees.

Deportation. A new word.

On the evening of 16 July 1942, they come to arrest my friends René and Bob's mother. Their father is an Aryan; she was born not in France, but in Germany, and she is Jewish.

We never see her again.

Mother says that they have arrested many, many people like her.

July 1942, vacation!

Mother tells me: "When you get to the corner of the
rue Boissonade, you must say: Phew! I'm hot, and take
off your jacket, so that the lapel folds over the star and
hides it. Then you must hold it naturally. Go quickly
past the concierges' lodge, but with a smile, because the
concierge there isn't to be trusted."

I carry out the instructions. Clo Avy-Prégniard,[6] widow
of the great artist Jean-Marius Avy, a friend of my grandfather's, who also painted, awaits us anxiously.

Promptly, she and Mother unstitch the stars from our
clothes and burn them to ashes.

We have lunch, and then, with Clo's blessing, we leave.

Repeat after me: I'm going to spend my holidays in La
Rochefoucauld, with my friends the Lalos. (As you really
have some friends called Lalo, and it's also the name of
the man who will help us escape, it all makes sense.)

I like the Lalo girls, twins in my class at school, very much; identical in every way except for the color of the ribbons in their hair.

Remember: we are going to pass the demarcation line, and join Uncle Daniel in the Unoccupied Zone. Our luggage has already left under the name of Monsieur Rouger, who offered us his help.

(I like my neighbors the Rougers, especially Nicole, who is my confidante.)

Be natural. Here we are at Austerlitz station. Smile, you're going on holiday. Don't touch your chest, there's no star any more.

Go ahead, walk through, climb up here, sit down.

The train pulls away, Mother looks at me and whispers "We did it! . . ."

Angoulême. We change trains. While we're waiting, we pace up and down the platform. A few travelers, a few German soldiers, armed.

The next train. Old, made of wood, with separate compartments. There's only one other passenger, who is smoking, smoking heavily, and his cigarettes make me feel sick.

Last year, I would have complained! Now I say nothing. I retch. Oh! The nauseating, bitter taste of this last journey as free citizens.

La Rochefoucauld. The train stops. Armed soldiers, lots of armed soldiers on the platforms.

Mother whispers to me: "This is the first time, it used to be a deserted little place."

We get out.

Identity card check at the exit.

"Go ahead, wait, go ahead, wait."

We wait, with a gentleman traveling on his own, a lady and her three grown up daughters.

When the travelers have all gone through, the soldier says: "Right, let's go"

We cross La Rochefoucauld. Dear God, I'm so small!

We go into a house, up some stairs, through a door.
    A large table: behind it, three or four officers, I don't remember, a soldier who is typing, and a dog! An enormous bulldog.
    Two officers ask us questions; one very gentle, smiling, courteous; the other brutal, shouting loudly. One after the other, like at the theater:
    "Who are you?"
    "Francine Christophe.
    18 August 1933
    106, rue Cardinet, 17th *arrondissement*, Paris.
    Father a lieutenant and prisoner of war."
    "You are Jewish."

"No."
"Say that you're Jewish, sweetheart."
"Admit it, little slut."
"Say it, pretty girl . . ."
"Spit it out, little monster!"
"Leave the room."

I am alone with a soldier, his rifle, and his dog.

Mother is next door with these men who shout or murmur.

I hear "No, no, no."

Then the door opens.

"Take a good look at your daughter, because if you don't admit it, we'll take her away."
    "Yes, yes, I'm Jewish."
    We go down the stairs, cross the square and go through a big doorway that closes behind us.

Mother looks at me and says:
    Phew!

And I start to cry because I know what that "Phew!" means: I'm in prison, but never mind, I don't have to hide any more, or cling to the shadows, run for my life, live in fear, dread what has now finally happened.

Fifty people surround us. They are all laughing, raising our morale.

Come on now, where there's life, there's hope. We've all been arrested, too bad. Let's make the best of it . . .

It is 26 July 1942.

Mother thinks our fake identity card was botched. And it's true. That's what alerted them at the station.

La Rochefoucauld does not have a prison, so we are housed in the Grain Exchange, in the function room, on the first floor.

Beds everywhere, even on the stage, where there are still a few theater props that make me laugh: a giant red boxing glove.

Some neighboring nuns prepare the food which we go in turn to collect twice a day.

A few policemen guard us and try to brighten our first moments as prisoners. One of them served under Uncle Charles. Mother asks him straight away to buy some tonic for me, and a towel. As he cannot find a towel, he brings one from his house, with his initials on it.

We stay for four days in La Rochefoucauld. On the last day, Mother arranges it so she goes to fetch the food, and gets two hard-boiled eggs from the nuns.

A coach brings us back to Angoulême.
    Angoulême. A real prison. Long corridors, huge doors, bars everywhere, the strict warden with her bunch of keys, the cells, the hatch in the door through which the billy can of thin soup and the quarter lump of sugar per day are passed.

Mother swills our shared room out with water when her turn comes, like the other prisoners (there is a very young lady with her baby).

The warden softens a little when she discovers this new type of prisoner she isn't used to.

For our washing and toilet needs, we go in groups into the courtyard, guarded by a sentry; a courtyard rutted and full of gravel, where building work is being done.

We can hear singing in the men's quarter.

All this interests me enormously.

We stay for four days in Angoulême, and every day, Mother gives me half a boiled egg.

We leave Angoulême in a coach.

Before we reach our destination (unknown to us all), we have a crash.

The people from the village give bread and butter to the children and get us sugar with their ration tickets.

Poitiers

My first camp. Divided in two with barbed wire, they put
Gypsies, whom they hunt down just like us, on one side,
and Jews on the other.

When we arrive, a rumor goes round: "Hide your wedding
rings, they confiscate them." Some put them in their
mouths. Mother slips hers into the knob of butter saved
from La Rochefoucauld.

We sleep in barrack-huts infested with rats, on straw
placed directly on the ground. One night, a rat runs over
my face. One lunchtime, plunging the ladle into the soup
cauldron, someone pulls out another.

The camp is swarming with people, the toilets with
worms. The toilets: a few cabins side by side, whose walls
and even ceilings are covered with these creatures. We
push them away with our feet before relieving ourselves
to avoid hearing the squishing noise they make beneath
our shoes.

After four days of rat soup, we leave Poitiers for an unknown destination.

In the middle of the night, guarded by armed soldiers and dogs, we are literally thrown into cattle wagons somewhere in the depths of the country. It's high and I hurt myself as I fall.

Doors closed and sealed. A soil-can in the center, quickly filled and overflowing.

People faint. Others vomit or become crazy. Children and old people cry. Everyone is suffocating.

The journey lasts for hours like this, in pitch darkness, with me pressed up against Mother.

Nauseating stench, thirst, hunger, fear, exhaustion.

Drancy, August 1942

I celebrate my ninth birthday here, among a succession of horrendous images that are stored and classified forever in my memory.

Drancy, a rectangle surrounded on three sides by unfinished high-rises, and on the fourth by a low brick building, which we call the "castle" and which contains about fifty toilet holes.

Next to that, an opening for arrivals and departures.

The dormitories: future apartments, half-finished.

We sleep on feather mattresses, bursting at the seams, encrusted with blood and excrement (where do these mattresses come from?) placed directly on the ground, which is crisscrossed with exposed pipes. We twist our ankles on them and feathers fly everywhere.

We can only visit the "castle" in groups of ten. Too bad about the diarrhea. (Please come, there are only nine of us and I can't wait any longer. I can't come, I already went a while ago and I'll be noticed.)

We cross the courtyard in single file, led by a gendarme, an immense courtyard, covered with slag, which makes it difficult to walk and sends out clouds of black dust. Our skin is grey.

Five high-rises loom over the camp, occupied by French gendarmes and their families. The gendarmes serve as wardens, some are terrible. The chief is atrocious.

Mother peels vegetables in the "cook-house" for hours at a time. Standing up. Among the vegetable peelers is a handsome, distinguished elderly gentleman whose memories help them forget their painful, sometimes bleeding, hands. He is a great musicologist and the ex-director of the Monte Carlo ballet. His name is René Blum, brother of Léon Blum[7] (he would die in Germany).

Oh! The herds of children filing by! Heads shaved, hollow cheeks, sometimes in rags, sometimes tied together with rope. Generally children of Central European Jews, automatically separated from their parents and mistreated, even in their country of refuge. The smallest can hardly walk, the older ones, maybe twelve or thirteen years old, help them. Herds of twenty, thirty, fifty, a hundred children. We ask them their names, their ages, and they don't reply. Beaten dogs, stunned, they have forgotten everything. They send them off to Germany. Sometimes, a few devoted women accompany them, their chests decorated with a star saying "Friend of the Jews."

Mother, do those who persecute little children like this kiss their own children at bedtime with a loving smile?

In the middle of the courtyard, a circle of barbed wire where those who are to be deported wait. A "search" hut, where other Jews, under the surveillance of policemen and German soldiers, must dispossess them of all their belongings.

And then they shave them, and tufts of hair of all colors fly among the grey clouds of slag.

Noise, shouting, whistles blowing, barking, roll calls, creaking.

They wait for the final journey seated on the ground, in the circle of barbed wire.
    A man with a shaved head gets up, sees a penknife on the ground and starts to shave his nails with it.
    Ah! So you can shave your nails with a penknife, sort of like peeling them; and this vision engraves itself on my memory.

Oh! More herds of children passing by . . .

Herds of sheep in the fields frolic a little. Herds of cows on country lanes stop to snatch a blade of grass. Herds of Jewish children in the camps have no soul left. They walk straight ahead, their eyes unseeing, slow, already dead.

"Oh! Mother, Mother, I can't look at them any more." I throw myself into her arms, cling to her as hard as I can, just like these little children must have clung to their mothers when they were taken from them.

I have seen some children with scratches all over their arms, because their mothers must have gripped onto them until their nails dug in.

And am I too on the way to the slaughterhouse?

Three weeks in Drancy. We wear the yellow star or risk imprisonment.

Then there are those who wear a white star on their chests on which they have written "Friend of the Jews."

Friends of the Jews, thank you.

It is here, amid all this misery, that I learn that I am a privileged little girl.

The Geneva Convention allows the wives and children of French prisoners of war to remain in France as hostages.

So, Father saves me from the unknown terror of the "great departure"; You, Father, whose nationality has not yet been taken from you, while for Mother and myself, it's already done, we are no longer anything, just JEWS. I still don't even understand what that means, and every day I repeat:
     "Why, Mother, why; tell me, Mother, explain . . ."

Pithiviers Camp

Lots of barrack-huts. Lots of police.

When we arrive, I find a four leaf clover in the grass. A sign?

I have forgotten what everyday life was like in this camp. I think we stayed there for two or three weeks. We meet up with my uncle Maurice Evrard (another name that need not have been declared, but how could we ever have imagined? . . .).

My only memory of this camp, but it's an overwhelming one, deportation. We have just become friends with Madelon Lang and her little boy. Pierre, their husband and father, is also a prisoner of war.

We don't have to leave, because we are privileged.

And yet at the morning roll call, my name figures on the list.
    A mistake, Mother explains to the gendarmes. "Bah! Let her go through the search, afterward you can try to get her back."

No, no, once you've been searched, it's over, no going back, you're part of the stripped, haggard herd that winds between the two barriers to the cattle wagons.

So, in this seething camp, in the early hours of the morning, among the crowds of people being pushed, shoved, and beaten, among the parcels, suitcases, and straw, among the hordes of young, old, sick, babies, stretchers carrying patients under sedation who are being taken anyway, begins a frantic race against time.

The mistake must be rectified before the train leaves.

Suddenly, Mother asks a gendarme with a kind face.
    "Do you know Colonel Charles Streiff?"
    "Indeed, I served under him in 19 . . ."
    "I'm his daughter-in-law, please save my little girl."

That evening, we wander, empty headed, in this huge, desolate, dirty camp, ferociously emptied of its some two thousand occupants.

Next to the search hut I see Darnand's young henchmen[8] loafing aimlessly, clad in black shirts. Boys of twenty, young people from my home town. Oh no! I feel ill, they have dispossessed, searched, molested the departing prisoners all day long.

In the barrack-hut, filled with things that the "departed" were keeping close to their hearts until the last moment, torn photos, handkerchiefs, and toys litter the ground.

Oh! The cattle wagons in which they transport us, doors and windows sealed, destination unknown, overflowing soil-cans, people stumbling, falling, swearing, moaning.

The interminable waits in railway sidings, to the sound of boots, voices, barking.

Three or four days to cover only fifty or so kilometers.

Hunger, thirst.
  Mother, protect me. Mother, I'm hot; Mother, I'm cold. Mother, is it true that I'm a dirty little Jewish swine?

Beaune-la-Rolande Camp, near Montargis

A camp emptied of all its occupants, children whose parents had already been taken.

For the first few days, there are Madelon and her son, Mother and myself. That's all.

Then there are so few of us that they put us all in the same barrack-hut, men and women, just separated by a partition.

For days and days, using ice-cold water, Mother and Madelon have to wash the blankets and mattresses soiled with vomit and filth by the convoy of children. This work was carried out under the scornful eyes of two nurses who, when they deemed that Mother and Madelon had done a good job, gave them a slice of gingerbread. Not long afterward, they leave Beaune-la-Rolande.

At midnight, on 31 December 1942, the men bang on the partition and wish us a Happy New Year.

Everyone laughs and sings.

"Please accept, Madame Christophe,[9] this modest gift,[10] with our warmest regards.

"May it forever bear witness to our heartfelt gratitude for the devotion you have always shown. May your self-sacrifice and overwhelming generosity in these trying times, in these most terrible conditions, be rewarded, and may the new year, in its infancy, be kind and favorable to you in sending back your dear prisoner, and may a healing peace then reign in your new-found home.

All your 'tenants' in barrack-hut 16b."[11]

Little by little, life in the camp gets organized . . . but the barrack-huts fill up, too.

I go back to being a little girl. Having almost forgotten life before the war (I was six years old when it was declared), having since lived with a growing and tenacious fear, the "calm" of Beaune-la-Rolande gives me a new equilibrium.

Of course, we are surrounded by barbed wire, armed guards survey us from their watchtowers, but there's no mention of dogs, which terrify me, nor imminent deportation.

And our wardens, honest customs officers from the Southwest of France, with their sing-song accents, brought here in spite of themselves to do this dirty work, help us as much as they can.

One of them, at great risk, brings me some apples in his haversack.

I only dislike one of them, who makes eyes at Mother. But Mother-and-Father are like the Republic, indivisible. So, one day when we're being searched (a frequent ceremony, regular and identical in all the camps) out of sheer disappointment, he turns over our suitcase in a rage, tossing everything around, ripping our hems.

Mother doesn't suspect I see what's going on, and that I love her even more for it.

Thanks to Mother, who has been appointed head of the barrack-hut, I learn how babies are born, when she cries "All hands on deck, women at the ready."

I also see a naked man for the first time, through an open door. It chokes me a little. I make this discovery accompanied by my new friend, a little girl of my own age, held here with her sister and mother, Ida Itelson.

We both adore a sort of giant with a shaved head "You'll see, that way I'll never be bald!" a very good man, whom we call Papa Leni, and his inseparable friend, as tall as he is and a gendarme (ruined by Vichy). One day, I say to Mother: "You know, he's not really called Leni, but Léni." Mother blanches, because she knows his name is Lévi and that he's going to try to get released for mistaken identity. In the meantime, he brings a paternal ray of sunshine into our lives, deprived as we are of our own fathers, since Odette's has been deported, and mine is a prisoner.

In our barrack-hut, the adorable elderly Madame Monte-fiore accepts her new-found state with the sense of humor and philosophy of a great lady.

Poem by Madame Montefiore in Mother's honor.
Barrack-hut 16.

New Year's Greetings, 1943

When we've had a painful fall,
Caught lice or even nothing at all
We look for Madame Christophe!
For a migraine, when we're homesick
To find some powder or a lipstick
A length of thread, a scrap of cloth.

To thankless sisters, on her part,
She opens her small case and big heart
To put an end to all our quarrels
Her scepter is a broomstick
Which sometimes disappears like magic
Among her subjects, ever rebels.

She can empty bins and ladle soup
Impose silence when to bed we troop
Command and bring us light relief
Glide her fingers on the piano keys
Even make our wardens pleased
And yet remain our chief.

When we push her too far and go on,
Abuse her kindness and so on
'Til we deserve a beating then, in brief
We must ask for her pardon
And shout together in unison
Hurrah for our barrack chief!

Also in our barrack-hut is a young woman with her two
tiny daughters. The camp food gives them worms, and
every evening their mother puts them over her knee,

bottoms in the air, to catch the worms: a curious sight that I never tire of watching.

In another barrack-hut, an elderly lady, an ex-stylist, tells us to keep the wrappings from our parcels. With them she makes astonishing hats with wide brims, a different one for everyone, full of imagination, which we all sport as soon as the weather gets fine.

Grandmother manages to send us a mess tin. What a joy not to have to eat out of the old pea tin we had kept since La Rochefoucauld.

And then we notice that behind the toilet huts, at the end of the camp, there are bunches of dandelions and wild lamb's lettuce. Wonderful. It brightens up the every day rations.

Camp law obliges us to wear our yellow stars nevertheless, but as the authorities don't send any, we are given paint and strips of calico, and we paint the stars using stencils.

BEAUNE-LA-ROLANDE. In my abnormal little girl's universe, this name symbolizes for me a kind of break, a resting place, a holiday! In brief, Beaune-la-Rolande was "good times"!!!

Since I no longer know what good times really are, here I blossom, I skip, I observe what I believe to be everyday life and I take under my protection several children who have lost their parents.

And I learn. The headmistress of my school in the rue Jouffroy manages, I don't know how, to send me some school books. Thank you, Madame Périn.

I throw myself into rehearsals for a matinee show organized by Max Viterbo, ex-director of the Cigale in Montmartre. Everyone exercises their talents: the singer Marguerite Solal, whose hit *"Je suis seule ce soir avec mes rêves"* ("I am alone tonight with my dreams") is imprinted on my memory forever.

A young girl is to dance the *bourrée auvergnate*, but as I also want to do a solo, I declare, stubborn as a mule, that I will dance the "real" *bourrée*.

Viterbo announces:
   "And now, Francine Christophe, in a 'personal' rendition of the *Bourrée Auvergnate*."

I'm very happy anyway. Everyone applauds. And I think that there, in Beaune, dancing on the table before the condemned prisoners who don't yet know it, my life's dream is formed: to perform in the theater.

Max Viterbo, Marguerite Solal and my "public," you find me entertaining, so much the better, you're going to die, but no one knows it.

We get ourselves organized.

Grandmother sends us parcels (how does she do it?). Aryan husbands and wives can visit their spouses through a wire fence.

Mother continues serving the soup and cutting the bread with the "lucky knife," taken from Grandmother's cutlery service before we left. It is beginning to wear out.

We come to find out all sorts of things.

First and foremost that Father is moving heaven and earth from inside his prison camp to get us released. Monsieur Scapini, an ambassador representing prisoners of war for the Vichy government (and who is blind, which allows him to see what is really happening in the camps!) has promised to help.

Others too. If all the people who are trying to get us released succeed, we'll be free at least ten times over! . . .

Uncle Charles is also looking after our release. As soon as he hears of our arrest, he leaves for Vichy, where Maréchal Pétain, whom he has known for a long time, agrees to see him.

Uncle goes into the office where Pétain, seated at his desk, is examining posters for Mother's Day.

Uncle speaks, explains, recounts. Pétain doesn't bat an eyelid. So Uncle, having run out of arguments, says: "But this is also about a mother and her child."

Philippe Pétain lifts his head: "Bah! Jews . . ." he says.

And so we are not released.[12]

After all, things aren't so bad here. I have almost enough to eat, I play with my friend Odette, I pick dandelions behind the toilets, I am an old hand in the camp. Even my cousin Pierre Nordmann comes to join us. Very tall, very blonde, very handsome, twenty years old. Dressed in a sheepskin jacket, taken at the Spanish border, trying to join de Gaulle's forces.

I catch lice and impetigo in my hair, which they cut as short as a boy's.

Unpleasant.

Mother's neck starts to swell up like a pillar. She no longer has her periods, like all the other women here, I might add. But periods don't concern me for the moment.

Mother has an attack of dysentery. The first . . .

In spite of everything, every morning, Mother hums a Maurice Chevalier song to herself:

In life it doesn't do to fret
I just don't have the time
'Cause life will get
Much better yet
And things will work out fine

I don't need to get upset
It's simply not my style
And you can bet
That I won't fret
I'll take it with a smile! . . .

The camp fills and fills . . . Working class people and high society. A whole community.

We make the acquaintance of Christian Lazard, the banker (his wife is Catholic), a good man, generous, refined, in golf pants and a flat cap, and Maître Valensi, with his famous moustache and infectious good humor.

Mother becomes a nurse. We live in the infirmary. A young man, a farm laborer, gets passed off as mad.

Ha ha! I took some lime-tree leaves from the infirmary, chopped them up very, very small, and with some toilet paper that had arrived in a parcel, I rolled some cigarettes. Behind the toilets, my friend and I savor the pleasure of smoking our first cigarette!

One morning, I wake up bright yellow. I have jaundice.

We change infirmaries, and Mother runs the new one.

One lady, Finaly the banker's sister, a poet under the name of Rosita, fakes madness, and her lawyer comes to fetch her in an ambulance.

I am very fond of Haas, the little doctor whose eyes sparkle mischievously, and Lévy-Baruch, the chemist.[13]

In the evening, before curfew, I pester and clamber all over Georges Nordmann, who is all patience and kindness. He is a legal counselor, distantly connected to my family, and married to an Aryan who is doing everything she can for him.

Beaune-la-Rolande camp February 1943

To my little friend Francine, concerning a lost glove.

Not knowing where, nor why, nor how,
For she's a dreamer as a rule,
Within the camp young Francine lost
A little glove of dark brown wool.

The school, wash-room, infirmary?
Or could it be in the canteen?
It disappeared without a trace
That glove belonging to Francine.

Without it's twin, the right glove mourned,
Wore out, became threadbare and torn,
And now when Francine's cold outside
Her pockets have to keep her warm.

Perhaps one day, but who knows when
A stroke of luck from up above,
Will help young Francine find again
Her little dark brown woollen glove.

Jeanne Montefiore, a.k.a. Grandmother

Barbed wire, yes, watchtowers, yes, but I can see apple-trees on the other side.

It's true, everything is all right here. Until the day the word deportation resounds in my ears.

Odette Itelson, her mother, her sister, Papa Leni, his friend the gendarme,[14] Viterbo, Marguerite Solal, Lazard the banker, Haas, Lévy-Baruch, Madame Montefiore, Pierre Nordmann, in short, everyone. I don't even know where they're going.

Even with hindsight, even racking my memory, I cannot remember anything else.

They all disappear from my life.

And I see lines appear on Mother's face.

We hear some more news. The Germans have gone to our apartment with a truck and taken everything, everything we did not have time to hide.

There's nothing left because, as is their habit, they take even the light sockets and switches, the finger-plates on the doors!

My doll's carriage, the last gift from Uncle Alfred, who won't be giving me any more . . .

Seeing the neighbors crowding round on the opposite pavement, watching the pillage, a German soldier fooled around, playing with my doll like a little girl.[15]

My head is exploding with unanswered questions. I turn
to Mademoiselle Rolland who helps cheer me up. Living
in Pithiviers, she is our go-between, untiring, always
smiling: all at once errand girl, postmistress, ambulance
driver, our link with the free world.

Also, from the Red Cross, Mademoiselle Monod visits
us and helps us too.

They send men married to Aryan women to the Atlantic
Wall, with the Todt organization.

Set to a popular tune ("Tout au fond de la mer, les pois-
sons sont assis"), here is my poetic effort for my tenth
birthday.

In our dear France so fair
There is a prison where (repeat)
All the poor Jews arrive
Most more dead than alive (repeat)
Ha! Ha! Ha!

Chorus:
Oh yes, to Beaune-la-Rolande camp
Oh yes, the wandering Jews all tramp
Tra la la la la la la, Tra la la la la la la

The whistle blowing at midday
Means the soup is on its way (repeat)
And everybody quickly runs
No need for trumpets or for guns (repeat)
Ha! Ha! Ha!

Every day at five o'clock
The roll call must be made (repeat)
The gendarmes come to count us all

Lest someone's been mislaid (repeat)
Ha! Ha! Ha!

In a corner of this camp,
The toilets can be seen (repeat)
And when you're walking past this place
The smell is quite obscene (repeat)
Ha! Ha! Ha!

Oh yes, to Beaune-la-Rolande camp
Oh yes, the wandering Jews all tramp
Tra la la la la la la, Tra la la la la la la

Sealed cattle wagons, overflowing soil-cans, dogs, guns, calls, cries. A whole day to cover the 100 or 150 kilometers from Beaune to Bobigny station.

Next stop the registration post in the Drancy courtyard, then the block.

I have been a prisoner for almost a year and I know the camps or prisons of:

La Rochefoucauld
Angoulême
Poitiers
Drancy
Pithiviers
Beaune-la-Rolande

Drancy again, Drancy-the-hell-hole, Drancy-the-crowded, Drancy-the-noisy, Drancy-the-louse-ridden, Drancy-the-bad-joke.

Seeing us arrive with our stenciled-on yellow stars, the internees rush up to us to take them off and distribute real ones, printed in black, marked with JEW in gothic letters. If you don't wear the proper star here, you risk imprisonment.

Drancy-the-Organized. A place for everything, everything in its place.

The more the months go by, the more Drancy turns into a model camp that everyone can admire, this neat dog-kennel that smells of resin, which we spread around by the bucketful (I can no longer bear the smell).

A month after our return to Drancy, Beaune-la-Rolande is emptied. Georges Nordmann is among those who return. I am filled with joy to see his warm smile again.

Lots of men leave for a work camp in Aurigny, in Normandy. They talk about the Aurigny work-house! Georges is among them. Maître Valensi too, and the Germans order him to shave off his famous moustache. No one remains more charming, pleasant, and gallant than he. With him, there's no victory for the Boche.

There are hundreds of children. The days of herds of children are gone. That was only for the foreigners! . . .

We are allowed to stay with our parents if we were arrested with them, even for the Great Departure.

To keep us busy, between roll calls and soups, the radiant Fania Perla, crowned with a thick brown plait, gathers us together and enchants us. She can do everything. With the help of the Haïm sisters, aged about eighteen, fifteen, and ten, and all three dancers and actresses at the Petit Monde theater, she puts on a show.

For a living tableau, I find myself teamed with Guy.

Oh! The handsome Guy, whose blonde hair and blue eyes, bordered with dark, curly lashes I noticed straight away.

My first childhood love, two years older than myself. We dance the Boccherini's minuet, looking into each other's eyes.

A Great Departure takes him away from me. One of those departures in the early hours of the morning, in Parisian buses, requisitioned and jam-packed. So one morning, I can no longer dance Boccherini's minuet.

We start a scout group. Songs, promises, good deeds for the day. The good deed could be to help an old lady to the toilets, carry soup to an invalid, help take care of a baby or even give a little of one's bread to someone even thinner.

We meet in the little courtyard behind our block, a court- yard with clay soil, with which we make little objects and leave them to dry in the sun. We can see freedom a hundred meters away! . . .

After a while, this courtyard is forbidden:

 – you could be seen from the outside and communi- cated with;

 – a gendarme shot at a prisoner;

 – there might be attempts to escape.

Escape! Our arrival in Drancy coincides, what's more, with a failed escape plan, a tunnel dug with great difficulty by a group of young men. When they are discovered, they are made to fill in the tunnel before being deported.[16]

And now I have seen my first dead body. He was hanging from a staircase, and I ran right into him. Ugly, rigid, poor man; the shock made me almost as rigid as he was.

Dead bodies, there are more and more of them. Invalids, those who had been badly treated when arrested, or tortured during interrogation, those overcome with emotion, and suicide victims, who would rather kill themselves than be deported.

A young man and his fiancée cut their wrists and threw themselves from a third floor window. I passed by a few moments later and the blood was still running on the ground.

Deportation, a mysterious word.

What is deportation? We devise theories. Some explain it in terms of gathering places, or work camps. Others speak of their premonitions.

Is it really worse than here? Is it worse than this reclusive life, crushed together in foul-smelling rooms, where the windows are painted over to conceal the freedom just the other side?

Is it worse than this hotchpotch of invalids, babies, pregnant women, old people, separated couples, broken families?

Does it mean more sick jokes, more deprivation, more lice, more blows?

We are housed in Block II, reserved for the "privileged." Our group of prisoners' wives and children grows. Made up of people from all backgrounds, all nationalities.

Lower, middle, and upper classes; lawyers', doctors', and intellectuals' wives, shopkeepers', artisans', and laborers' wives.

There is even a lady who . . . does something bad for a living, say my girlfriends.

All these people, saved by the power of a prisoner husband, whether an officer or a private. And then there are a few women hidden among us whose husbands are not prisoners but are deported or in hiding, members of the Resistance or dead and who, thanks to fake letters and papers, thanks to their courage and cool heads, have found a way to escape deportation.

Some of our companions, arrested as members of the Resistance, are sent to us on discovery of their Jewish origins. One of them, indeed, comes from Fort de Mont-Luc.[17]

I remember passages from a song that she wrote to a popular tune at the time of her arrest:

> *They drag me from my home*
> *Just like everyone else*
> *For reasons quite unknown*
> *Just like everyone else*

They search my bags and worse
Without a by-your-leave
They relieve me of my purse
Without a by-your-leave

Lord! I got such a fright
With the Gestapo tonight
Without a by-your-leave

Strangely enough, at Drancy, I forgot my age. Very old,
very young. Very young and especially very hungry to
finish the leftovers of little Josette's soup. Arrested at
the age of four or five months, I believe; she was saved
three times from death, once thanks to bottles of oxygen
miraculously brought in from outside.

A blonde, pink little doll, frail, pretty, and fragile, she
nibbles at her food. And my robust stomach impatiently
awaits the meals Josette doesn't want, when I know her
mother Odette Weill, from Nancy, will give me her daughter's leftovers.

I feel very old, if I think of my life in rue Cardinet. But I
think about it less and less.

I make friends with a girl of my age, Myriam Baur, tall and
beautiful, from a well-educated family.
    Myriam has several brothers and I envy her; her father
lives here with her, and I envy her even more. The Baur
family, devout believers, introduce me to the Jewish religion, and I admire it; but it doesn't take a hold on me, for
I do not have a religious inclination.

For her mother's birthday, while my friend makes her a
heart made out of dried clay found in the small court-

yard, I give her the Tables of the Law, made from the same dried earth.

With my theatrical leanings, I strike sad poses when my friend speaks of her father, when mine is so far away. In fact, during this period, I don't miss Father, or even Mother, when her occupations take her away from me for whole days at a time.

I'm turning into an animal who thinks only of its empty stomach. Come, come, Francine, react, or else it's a sure sign that the Boche are winning.

My young friend belongs in Block III, for the "big shots," the envy of all. From the balconies they take to go back to their dormitories, you can glimpse freedom!

And you can sometimes communicate by sign language with the free world!!! Another of my friends lives there too; the Daniel family, with three children, whose father officiates at the synagogue.

Yes, I did say synagogue.

For Drancy has to become a model camp, Drancy has to be visited and admired! Drancy, the transit point for migrating Jews, the "gathering place," has to have a synagogue.

The rabbi (the former Chief Rabbi of Lyons) is young, dynamic, full of new and modern ideas. He gives us religious instruction, teaches us canticles, and tries to instill in us a respect for mankind and goodness. I still have glowing memories of this smiling man, with his collar-like beard, which the Germans make him shave, against his religion.

(One day, I asked him if the Good Lord knew we were there. But I left before hearing his reply.)

Mother gets herself taken on at the "cook-house," as during our first stay here. The chef has to search the vegetable peelers.

Once, Mother told him:
"Monsieur Georges, please don't search me too thoroughly. Every day, I take (and will continue to take) a few potatoes, which I put in my sleeves. We shall both keep quiet; up there, I have children who retch at the sight of the never-ending soup . . ."

It's true. We aren't even hungry. As a result of eating this boiled and re-boiled soup, our teeth clench just at the smell of it.

A young man with sparkling black eyes has just arrived.
"You remember the Joan of Arc acting classes," says Mother, "I was sixteen and used to stroke your curly baby locks."

His name is Robert Manuel; his recent graduation from the Conservatory and his entry into the Comédie Française had not gone unnoticed.

Ah! How lovely Drancy is. We replace the black slag with cement laid by the prisoners. The center of the main courtyard, where shorn hair used to fly, brightens in the sun with green grass.

And the organization! The clothing store run by a white-haired gentleman, before whom Rose-Marie Leriche, our companion, loses both her countenance and her turban:

she had filled a scarf with paper to give her hair volume on top, as is the fashion, and it all fell off.

The cook-house, through which tons of rutabagas pass, and whose chef I admire because a birth defect favored him with six fingers on each hand!

The infirmary, served with devotion by men such as Dr. Gilbert Dreyfus who, paralyzed in one arm, is doubly active with his good arm.

The offices, the administration, the chancery (*Kommandatur*), the prison cells, the synagogue, the theater, a whole town, really!

A town where they scream at night in the prison cells, like Monsieur Oppenheimer, for example, whom they beat every evening, then sluice with ice-cold water and leave all night, naked and soaking wet. His brother wanted to escape. They died, the Oppenheimer brothers, one in Drancy, the other in Germany.

A town where you have to drop your pants when you arrive and show that you're not circumcised in order to regain your freedom. Ah! I remember one young man who, for the Germans, had a typically Jewish physique; I can still see him doing up his buttons as he comes out of the Chancery, laughing with joy at the freedom they'd promised him, once he'd sworn he was an Aryan. How wise his parents had been! How many I see coming out of the Chancery bent double in pain from the kicks they have received.

A town full of talents and Conservatory first prizes: violinists, pianists, virtuosos, singers, actors, opera composers like Marcel Lattès. Mother, who studied with Margaret Debrie, the sculptor's daughter, and auditioned before Lazare Lévy, plays the piano. Thus the Germans select her to figure in a film that must show Drancy-Paradise to the whole world. Chopin, Liszt, Beethoven etc. Anything and everything to entertain those who are leaving!!!

Those who are leaving . . .

Mother disappears for hours on end. When she returns to the dormitory, defeated and exhausted, she collapses onto the straw mattress.

What does she do?

Under Monsieur Alphen's orders, she is first the assistant for the "waiting staircase." then second-in-command for the "departure staircase."

The waiting staircase, the staircase of hope. Doubtful cases, litigious cases. All those whose Spanish, Swiss, or even English origins have a chance of saving them. They're all waiting for a document, a declaration, a visa, who knows, that will get them out.

Unlike Pétain's government, the English never cease to proclaim that an Englishman, Jewish or not, is an English-man. Consequently, their citizens can be imprisoned, of course, since they are at war, but with the respect due to all subjects of the King, and not deported. Many are sent to Vittel, where a camp has been set up for them.

As for the Spanish, they imprison Jews on their own territory (the lesser of two evils) or generously hand over to the Germans the French Jews whom they pick up at the border (as in the case of my cousin Pierre). On the other hand, they save many of their own nationals.

The Swiss also save many of their compatriots, when they can. (It is rumored that the Swiss Germans make more effort than the Swiss French.)

We all think with admiration of the King of Denmark who, it is said, wore the yellow star on the day that his Jewish subjects had to wear it and succeeded in getting them evacuated to Sweden.

And to think that I used to sing "Marshall, here we are."
    I think of my elderly uncles and cousins who fought at Verdun and are not on the waiting staircase but on the one for those who are leaving . . .

The departure staircase.

Reserved for those heading for the unknown. Crushed together, sorted, counted, compressed, re-counted, re-sorted, unable to leave the staircase.

They know they are leaving. Some resign themselves, others shout, others pray, others plead "save me."

Young, old, babies, invalids, couples, entire families; already strained by several months in the camp, or newly arrested; tortured, molested, or well-treated; defeated or rebellious; dazed or full of themselves; no mercy.

Pregnant women in pain, suicide attempts in a coma, tuberculosis sufferers, and even once, thirty children with scarlet fever.

A list is a list. Even the baby hidden under a mattress. They recount until they find him, because he's been numbered. A number is a number. German bureaucracy is unbeatable. Several times, Monsieur Alphen says to Mother, who had stayed behind to help people: "Run quickly to your room, Madame Christophe, the list is incomplete. They'll take the first passer-by."

Some of those who are leaving are unaware, others suspect that they are going to die. Some entrust us with messages, notes, small objects that are dear to them.

To Madame Christophe,
That Rare Smiling Providence in the Camp of Tears,
Drancy, November 1943.

Maurice Level, who is leaving.

Oh heaviness among all others!
Barbed wire our every dream invades
This world so close and filled with rumors
Into the distant silence fades.

Six verses . . .

Jostling from one level to the next, cries, appeals, resuscitation for those who have fainted, children's tears, the crush of parcels, straw mattresses, the clang of containers, a thermos for a newborn, Solucamphor for a cardiac sufferer, a blanket for the man who just came out of the dungeon and is shivering; in the middle of this seething mass, this panic, this racket, someone sometimes finds a brother, a cousin, a friend.

On days like that, for example when they bring in her

cousin Albert Heymann, who has just got out of the Rothschild hospital, Mother returns to the dormitory even more defeated. I see her in the distance, crossing the courtyard and dragging her feet. On days like that, she even loses a little of her patience with me if, for example, I haven't put out her plate or made the bed.

And I am resentful.

On the departure staircase, you get some very dark looks. They seem to say, "So you, you're staying! You're staying. Why you?"

And Mother feels almost guilty. Yes, why her? Sometimes I feel that. Even more rarely, I rebel, with my childish selfishness.

"I want my mother for myself. And I want my father too. I'm ten years old and I love to laugh."

But usually, I just live for the present moment, thinking less and less. I wait for my soup, I wait for bedtime.

Little by little, as their leaders disappear, the various movements do the same: the scouts, the theater, religion, everything goes.

After 11 November 1942, the invaded Unoccupied Zone surrenders its cargo of refugees. All those who believed themselves secure in Pétain's safekeeping. The transportations increase. A few more foreign Jews who had been hidden either by Christians, or by French people of their own faith. (Until the end, there were Jews who really believed that only those who had done something bad, like the black market, for example, got arrested.)

Mount Auburn Hospital

Pay Station Number	9
Entered:	01/21/2020
	15:12
Exit:	01/21/2020
	16:08
Ticket Number:	55324
Transaction Number:	270175
Rate:	A
Parking Fee:	$4.00
Total Tax:	$0.00

Total Fee:	$4.00
Fee Paid:	$4.00
Visa	
XXXXXXXXXXXX1231	
Approval Number:	058660

Thank you for your visit
Please come again!

But especially French people. We still see them pouring in with their little bundles. We even see them arriving frozen and ill, picked up on the Southern beaches in their swimming suits, not allowed to get dressed.

And we start seeing unaccompanied children again too, those who had been hidden by their parents or entrusted to Jewish resistance groups, scattered between a few convents and Catholic families, but especially among the Protestants of regions like the Isère and the Cévennes. (The fact that the Protestants went out of their way to help us can be explained by their own minority condition, so often persecuted throughout the centuries.)

Babies, little girls and boys, betrayed for the money, or sometimes for nothing, for pleasure, arrested with the young clandestine Jewish scouts in charge of hiding them.

Alice the mother, Simone the daughter, two of Father's cousins find themselves face to face with Mother in the waiting staircase. True Christophes, they must both be at least six feet tall!

"My dear Marcelle, I beg you," says Alice, "one of my feet is killing me. Please find me a chiropodist. I can't leave like this!" ("Where does she imagine she's going?" thinks Mother.)

Never mind, she visits all the dormitories, raising her hand to her mouth:

"Is there a chiropodist here?"

She brings one back. Alice, relieved, was able to leave . . . Simone too. Engaged to a Catholic, a ring on her finger might have saved her. But the ring wasn't yet on her finger . . .

The waiting staircase, roll calls, pounding hearts, transfers to the departure staircase.

They leave in the early hours of the morning. The Parisian buses fill up in an indescribable crush and racket. Children, elderly people, and paralytics have to be carried. In the central alleyway, coma victims and those who have just given birth are laid out. Dogs, whistles blowing, insults.

The departure staircase is deserted, gloomy, filthy, scattered with rubbish, the evidence of so many tragedies, it must be cleaned quickly, and then wham, the next batch arrives.

After almost a year at Drancy, it's out of the question for me to make friends with anyone. There's no time any more.

The Germans send several women from our group to the Levitan furniture shop. Their job is to pack up the Jewish goods, for dispatching to Germany. Sometimes, one of the women comes back crying, "I packed up my silverware today." Another, with a sense of humor that is as sharp as ever: "Today, I recognized my Mother-in-law's dining room suite. Ha, ha! I always hated it."

As for me, I know that my big doll has passed through Levitan's, then on to the Gare de l'Est. I wonder what the little German girl who plays with it is like.

Ah! Block III, the "big-shots'" block. One day, we learn that the men in Block III will be allowed to go out for whole days at a time in Paris! To go out in Paris?

Yes, but in the evening, they must return to the camp accompanied by a Jew they have arrested themselves . . .

The first ones to give a false address, and of course to get caught, a father and son whom Mother knows, are deported.

One night, the British Air Force comes to bomb Bobigny station. An airman parachutes down from a plane that was hit, just next to the camp!

All night we see the buildings and warehouses of Bobigny burning. That makes us laugh, but the sound of the anti-aircraft guns makes me shiver.

Ah! Block III. Not cut out to be policemen. One day, everyone is sent to the departure staircase. I like you so much, my little friend Myriam Baur. You disappear like Guy.

Everything disappears. Everyone disappears. I start to be afraid again, like before I was arrested. With a fear that hurts my stomach.

We all go before the camp chief, S. S. Brunner. With our papers, letters, everything that proves that we are really the wives and children of prisoners. Several women are afraid their deception will be discovered. But their fake letters are properly done.

For proof, Mother shows the photo of Father, sent from his first camp. A small group of bearded officers, puffed up by the newspaper that keeps them warm under their pea jackets.

We felt so sorry for Father when we got that photo, and now we're just like him!

How thick Mother's neck is!

The latest arrivals at Drancy have come from the former Unoccupied Zone, now ransacked, surrounded, grid-mapped. They look like hunted animals, and indeed I hear people whispering terrible tales of manhunts.

Some, who have just been arrested in the lunatic asylums where they were hiding, are naturally mentally exhausted after so many months of horrendous play-acting. Others, rooted out from cellars and caves, had felt the chains tightening around them. Men who were betrayed, sold, bartered.

And still more unaccompanied little children, entrusted to convents by their parents before they themselves were arrested, and looked after by the Jewish resistance groups. Once the parents had been arrested and the resistance groups disbanded, there was no more money to pay for their keep, so several doors opened . . . and those of Drancy close.

We're Leaving

We're leaving, that is, we're leaving our country. I have to get that into my head. Mother seems to find this only fair. "Always someone else, why not me."

She reminds me of our arrest: "Phew! The chase is over." I, however, am used to being privileged.

Privileged I stay. Nothing like the others' departure. The Geneva Convention still protects us a little. We keep our luggage and our clothes, and we pack up as much as possible of the food we had received in our parcels.

No buses for us. Trucks covered with tarpaulins. I watch Paris through the little rope holes. How I love you, Paris. Wide, bright, calm, with no traffic. You forget quickly in two years.

The trucks stop and we get out.

The Gare de l'Est.

We are pushed under the pillars and we wait there, standing, for a long time, with our parcels around us, and the smallest children want to run around. The soldiers guarding us have guns.

The pedestrians around us slow down, or stop to look at this troop of 100 or 150 women and children.

Oh Mother! How I wish I could tear this star off. I don't want people looking at me like that any more. I want to go away. Why are there guns? Make these people go away. I'm not an animal.

I stamp my feet.

"Look, darling" says Mother, "these people who are stopping, they want to hold their arms out to you."

But they don't.

Madeleine Dreyfus tries to run away, but she fails.

Rose-Marie Leriche who speaks German no longer wants to. She says to one of our guards, older than the others:

"It's despicable what you're doing."

"We'll be punished one day . . ."

We squash into third-class carriages attached to the normal train. People even go along our corridor to get to the restaurant car.

We still have a little money, and this same restaurant car agrees to sell us drinks!

The last time I traveled in a passenger carriage, it was to go south. This time I'm going north.

I even go so far north that I visit a little bit of Belgium. The Meuse. Apparently in the midst of these terrible mountains, Albert, the King of the Belgians, killed himself.

When I think of the cattle-wagons, what a wonderful journey!

Mother smiles grimly at me. The others too.

Me too, in the end.

I have left you, my country.

I'm in Germany. I'm in Germany, I'm in Germany. Mother says to me: "It's better for our morale. Being a prisoner on your own home ground is harder."

We cross a destroyed Cologne. Since the border, we have been constantly changing guards. More and more terrible.

There it is, I'm starting to be afraid again. In the pit of my stomach.

Hanover. We get out of the train.

An air raid. We go down into the station cellars, while the bombs explode.

Civilians move up to make room for us.

What a crowd in there. Ourselves, civilians, armed soldiers.

Everything trembles. Me too. Everything creaks as if it were about to fall down. Sounds blur together, bombs, anti-aircraft guns, machine guns, voices, tears.

The air raid ends, we get back onto the train. The guards have changed.

We travel on and on. At Celle, we stop and change trains again; they push and shove us, squash us in, mothers, children, parcels, pell-mell, no time to catch our breath.

Civilian guards with long leather coats. Whenever I see those long leather coats, my legs turn to lead.

I'm beginning to understand the German insults.

We travel on. When we arrive at Belsen, we get out.
 Roll call. We don't understand our names very well, pronounced with a German accent. Kristofer Vrannziner. Kristofer Marzeler. They shout at us to get into the trucks.

7 May. Barbed wire. More barbed wire.

Bergen-Belsen

A large central roadway, and on each side, enclosures
separated by barbed wire. Barrack-huts in each enclosure.
People looking at us. And what looks!

Our enclosure. The barrack-huts. Our barrack-hut.

The others run toward us, avid for news. Dutch, Greek,
and Germans. Also privileged like us, since they still have
their hair and their clothes.

With the help of all our languages mixed together, they
ask us for news and food! . . .

The barrack-huts contain a large stove in the middle,
long tables and benches, and wooden bunks, three beds
high. It's the first time I've seen three-story bunks; up
until now, I'd only seen two. We plump up the straw in
the mattresses, so there is room at the end of the bed to
squeeze in our suitcases. We sleep with our feet on them.

Our first soup at Bergen-Belsen. The other prisoners

astonish us by gulping it down, along with ours, which we gladly give them. How can they eat it? The herbs it's made of are in there with their roots, unwashed, and the dirt crunches between your teeth. We make do with our black bread and the knob of margarine and provisions brought from France.

Over the road, the enclosure opposite is full of Russian prisoners of war. They say that they starve them completely.

I try to make friends with the Dutch children, but we can't seem to understand one another.

"What are you called?"

"Call, call, *morgen*."

"No, no, your name"
•
"No, no, *ja*."

"If we have to stay here for long, maybe you should learn German." says Mother, "It could be useful."

A Dutch lady gives me lessons.

A second convoy from France joins us. The women who worked at Levitan.

Now it's our turn to eat the soup that disgusts them!

I'd gladly eat twice as much of it.

This convoy also brings us Henriette Mala's oldest son, for she had been arrested with only her two youngest children.

Toinon's three children too. (She had hidden them, then was arrested and managed to escape. When she went to join them in their hiding place, she was told that they'd just been taken. So she went to give herself up to find them.)

Also Monsieur Reinach, State Councilor, nephew of the writer d'Appolo, and his wife.

And Monsieur Meyer, the mayor of Le Havre, his wife and her daughter, who was a nurse during the "funny kind of war."

And Pierre Ogouz, a journalist and a great collector of autographs, his wife, and his mother.

They call us the "hostages."

A letter from Father!! Sent to Bergen-Belsen!![18]

"11 June 1944. My poor dear darling. So there you are in Germany with our little girl. They've brought us closer together, so every cloud has a silver lining. I've had a terrible month since I got Madame Tcherka's letter of 1 May; I had heard nothing since 20 April. Kahn wrote to his brother telling him of the direction you had taken; imagine how I felt; it was only yesterday evening that I learned of your address in a letter from Mother dated 3 June. I also hope that you will be able to reply. I will move mountains to make this happen. Tcherka is also writing to his wife; he is well, I was the one who told him. Never forget that you are the wife of a prisoner of war; and that the Geneva Convention allows us to correspond, since it specifies the POW's close family, and this particular POW has no closer family than his wife and children. Be brave, my darling, and patient; keep your hopes up, don't be discouraged; happiness will return. Remember how happy we were, just 5 years ago in June 1939. Tell me how long your journey lasted and in what conditions. Did you and the little one get through it all right? How do you live and sleep and eat? What do you do during the day? If you and the little one are together, does the Geneva Red Cross look after you and bring you food? Do you have books and newspapers? Who are the other prisoners, are there men too? Is there a canteen and do you need money, in which case I will request authorization to send you some German marks? Mother, who's being very brave and optimistic, is well, me too. Kiss Francine for me, keep your good humor, I have never loved and admired you so much as today.[19] Robert."

No, even a prisoner of war could not imagine what a concentration camp was like.

Immense pine forests surround the camp. They seem dark, deep, terrifying.

The troops do their exercises there. We see them filing by chanting "*Hali, halo*" through the barbed wire.

As for Mother, every morning she hums her little song. I guess at the murmured words that escape from her mouth:

In life it doesn't do to fret
I never have the time

'Cause life will get
Much better yet
And things will work out fine

Yes of course, Mother!

The men and women leave every day to go and work in
kommandos.

The children stay in the camp. We drift around, we play,
between roll calls and soups, the milestones of peniten-
tiary life.
    They make Mother barrack-nurse. She tries to spare her
weakest charges from the *kommandos*, but doesn't always
succeed.

I have so many lice that she cuts my hair shorter than
a boy's. I'm so scared they'll shave my head. She cuts
my friends Monique and Arlette's hair as well, and then
almost all the girls' hair. We scratch so hard.

Our first shower at Bergen-Belsen; the showers are a long
way away from our enclosure. You have to walk for a long
time down the central road.

We go naked into a big room and hang our clothes on the
trolleys that carry them to be disinfected.

Several women put their hands in front of them, embar-
rassed because it's the first time their sons have seen
them naked. Sons of fourteen or fifteen.

We go down a long corridor where an S.S. guard is waiting
at the end.

We wait for an hour in the room, naked, until the shower heads spit out some water. Officers pass from time to time to look.

The women who work in the *Kommandos* are now sorting silk worm cocoons. In the evening, they bring back some of the cocoons, which we mount on sticks to make animals or funny little figures.

We have more and more lice. Not fleas like in France, but more and more head lice and body lice, recognizable by the twisted crosses on their backs. Boche lice, in short.

We crunch them between two thumbnails.

When the "grey mice" who watch over us give us orders, they shout "bloody do this, bloody do that!"

So one day Mother turns round and shouts in fury to a fellow prisoner who speaks German: "Tell them they must be treating us like this because they're only used to seeing German prisoners' wives! . . ."

The Russian prisoners opposite have disappeared. In their place, deportees in striped uniforms.

What's more, in all the surrounding enclosures, we see nothing but deportees with striped uniforms and shaved heads. Sometimes with letters or signs painted on their backs.

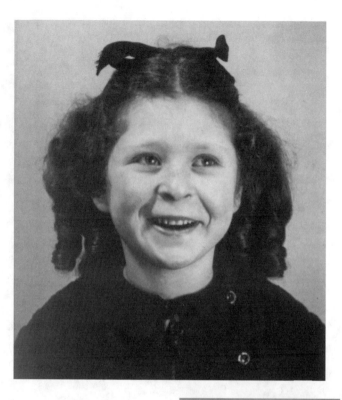

Francine in 1941.

Francine, n.d.

Robert and Francine.
Lieutenant Christophe's
first leave. Nice 1939.

Francine and Marcelle.
Like the soldiers, Francine
is wearing an army cap.
Promenade des Anglais,
Nice 1939.

Francine and Marcelle
before their arrest, 1942.

Dessiné le Rolande 1942

Une Colombine   Un pierrot.

22 ans   22 ans

Portrait of Francine
Christophe at age 10. Watercolor by an anonymous
prisoner who died at
Auschwitz. Beaune-la-Rolande
concentration camp, 1942.

Drawings by Francine. She will
only draw couples because
her parents are separated.
Angoulême prison, 1942.

Francine's song for her tenth
birthday, 1943.

Drawing of Drancy
concentration camp.

Robert Christophe.
Watercolor painted at
Oflag XVIIA, Austria.
Robert sent this to his
mother-in-law, who
forwarded it to Marcelle
at Beaune-la-Rolande
concentration camp.

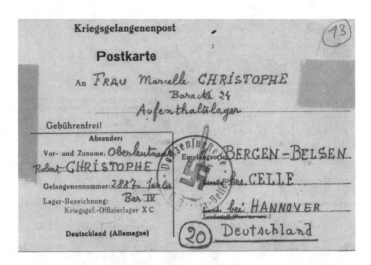

Postcard from Robert to Marcelle Christophe, 1944. Robert and Marcelle had to write each other in German or their correspondence would not be delivered by their German captors.

In the morning, we drink beetroot juice. At midday, rutabaga soup. In the evening, rutabaga soup. In the soup, a few little cubes of meat float (dog, from the dog abattoirs not far from the camp, so they say).

We go to fetch this soup in enormous cauldrons, which are much too heavy. The forty liter ones have to be carried by two people, and it's so hard! The twenty-five liter ones also need two people, but we make up teams of four people to carry three containers, then we change arms, and it's a bit easier.

Mother said the other day as she put the cauldron down: "something just cracked in my back."

With big ladles, we stir the soup right to the bottom so that everyone gets some vegetables or a cube of meat. Cubes of about two centimeters. Mother gives me hers. I glance at my neighbors' plates to see if they have more than I do.

A large square black loaf per week per person and a square of margarine.

At night, sometimes, we hear cries.

The dead are burned in cremating ovens. We can see the chimneys as high as factories.

The women come back from the *kommandos* rejoicing.

"They've landed."

We get out the tables, in the alley between two barrack-huts. We stand on them and shout:

"They've landed." I'm just hungry.

Tell me Mother, how far away is the landing?

The summer arrives, with its burning sun and terrible heat.

Big, black insects stick to our skin. You have to hit them to get them to fly away. They call them German flies.

We drip with sweat. The dead bodies instantly smell terrible.

It's the fourteenth of July. Henriette Mala has a red dress, others some white or blue clothing. Several of our companions dress in blue, white, and red and parade around the camp or go dressed like that to the *kommandos*. Nothing is said, and the prisoners from the other enclosures look on with joy and fright.

Claude Tcherka's idea: on 20 August, for Madame Christophe's birthday, the children will organize a "party" in the evening, in secret. The "party" takes place and ends with the chorus of the French provinces.

Privileged. French women and their children. Some Dutchwomen, mostly diamond cutters from Antwerp. Some Greeks, almost all from Salonica, the only Jews to escape from Greece. Many speak French, having studied at the French lycée. Some Germans.

Among the group of French women there are a few Polish women whose husbands had served in the French Army.

Even a Hungarian woman, who managed to keep her
boots and dance a wild *czardas* for 14 July.

In our barrack-hut, the beds are grouped in blocks,
like blocks of houses. We group together according to
affinities. The French together, for example. It's a question
of language.

We have terrible discussions with the "Polaks" who don't
understand why we don't speak Yiddish.

"You Jewish, no?"
   "Yes, I'm Jewish, since I'm here."
   "So you must speak Yiddish."
   "Not at all. Where could I have learned it?"
   "So you not Jewish."

It goes on like this for hours.

Ah! When Hitler spoke of the "the Jewish race," what a
blunder he made.

We recognize other French people immediately.

The Dutch (we call them the rot-rots, rasping the r's, because of their rather guttural language) are true Northern Europeans. They cut their bread "Dutch style," as
thinly as Dutch cheese, and they are serious people,
hard-working and obstinate.

The Greeks, swarthy and fatter than we are, even though
they are starving; their women cry like Middle-Eastern
mourners.

The Germans are Germans and proud of it. They are the most deeply shocked among us. So patriotic and so utterly betrayed.

Those who come from Eastern Europe are different. They've lived with pogroms from generation to generation. They are simply Jewish.

If one day they have a country of their own, how they will love it!

I talk about all this with my two red-headed friends, whose red-headed mother has decided to teach me Yiddish so we can chat together, because we're very fond of one another.

She is very kind, but all I can remember is that I am *eine grosseu na* (a great blockhead) and that I have *ein grossen toureuss* (a big behind). Because in spite of my thinness, my behind remains well padded.

I'm forgetting the Hungarian group, defended for a long time by the regent Horthy (a terrible dictator, but not too anti-Semitic). And then the Albanian group, who arrive from the mountains, with piercing eyes, fur hats, peasant-like (I view them a bit like savages).

I have my likes and dislikes.

I do not like Madame X . . . (my friends say that she hides food under her mattress, and we roam around her bed). We call her son the banshee, because he's always wailing.

I adore Madame Jacobi whose two sons are so handsome, especially Toli, the oldest, with whom I get on so well.

And I like Nana, and Rose-Marie, whose son, the adorable three year old Michel, is the love of my life.

Mother only uses the familiar *tu* with Madelon, whom we have known since Beaune-la-Rolande. Father and Pierre, her husband, live in the same prison camp and are great friends.

Madelon keeps a photo of Jean-Claude, her son, taken when they were arrested, at the age of three. The most beautiful, curly-haired baby you could imagine.

Now, Jean-Claude, who is terribly thin, won't eat any more. He keeps a mouthful of food between his teeth all day. And I'm so hungry it drives me crazy to see him refuse his food. I want to take his soup from him. When I pass behind him, I pinch him to punish him for not being hungry.

Once a week, we're given bread soup. If you keep it until the next day, it goes hard like a flan. If you close your eyes, it's delicious, like cake.

The summer passes and everywhere is filled up. And yet there are so many dead!

Mother is elected head of the barrack-hut.

It annoys Mother to see the children wandering around aimlessly all day, in every nook and cranny, when the women are working in the *kommandos*.

She's gripped by fear when we approach the barbed

wire, for the sentries can always shoot from up in the watchtowers.

She has an idea. Sit down around me, she says.

In her hand she has Father's first book, *Dona Conception's Terrific Adventure.*[20]

We listen open-mouthed, breathless, and enchanted.

She tells us that when Father wrote this book, she begged him: "Robert, please, make it have a happy ending. Don't make her die."

Dona Conception doesn't die and we breathe a sigh of relief.

"What a wonderful film it would make," says Claude Tcherka, one of the boys, "but why do you keep leaving bits out?"

I cannot give an opinion, as I've never been to the cinema.

Mother reads to us, either around a table, or outside, around a ditch, with our feet swinging above it.

After Dona Conception, *Bazaine the Innocent*. I think this fascinates us even more, maybe because it's about injustice, of which we are so much the victims.

The square where they take the roll call. These roll calls last for hours, standing up, lined up by barrack-hut. There are always mistakes: those who are sick or dead, even whole *kommandos*, are forgotten.

And they have to start counting again, until they find the mistake.

It can last for two hours, three hours, four hours. In the scorching sun, standing to attention.

Now it's not so hot, I don't wander around so much.

One S.S. officer has a harelip that has been operated on, and we call him "Harelip" among ourselves.

During one roll call, he points to a friend's mouth and says:
    "What have you got there?"

"The same horrible thing as you!"

He turns on his heel without replying.

He is bearable. But his stepbrother, who is much more terrible, is never seen without his riding crop.

The worst one is "Rote" Muller, so-called because he is all red. He screams his orders. I'm terrified of him.

For our showers, we carefully save the little soap we still have left. We soap our hair with delight. But suddenly, they turn the boiling water on, and we jump out of the way to avoid getting burnt, or else, just when we're covered with suds, the water stops. The S.S. pass by and snigger.

Our greatest pleasure, in the evening, after lights-out, is to go to a restaurant.

"This evening, I'm taking you to Chez Janine, a bistro in my *quartier*. Let's start with the house *andouillette* (tripe sausage), my husband's favorite."

Mother invites us to the Cabaret, in rue Marbeuf, which we discovered thanks to Uncle Alfred (here we sat next to the top officers of the *Wehrmacht*, who didn't know they were brushing shoulders with two Jewesses and a member of the Resistance, also Jewish to boot).

But the best dinners are provided by Mérika Bourgas, a sort of monument with flaming hair, who has seen everything, experienced everything.

She takes us to Maxim's, the Tour d'Argent, which none of us has ever been able to afford.

I fall asleep with my mouth full of chocolate profiteroles, under the fond gaze of the maitre d'.

I wake up very happy because Mother, always full of ideas, spoils me with one of her special sandwiches: a slice of raw rutabaga, topped with cooked rutabaga.

The cold becomes raw and stinging. We make an inventory of our store of clothing. Shoes are the shortest in supply.

The *kommandos* are now working on taking apart the German army's boots. Sometimes they get us boot bottoms, which make perfect clogs when they're filled with paper.

But paper is short, and the *"Kommandos"* bring us green-grey uniform cloth (which comes from the blood-stained clothing returning from the Front) and we make slippers with it. We drag our feet a little when we walk, because they're heavy, but at least our feet are dry.

We keep a piece of cloth from which we gently draw threads, one by one, when we need to repair something.

Everyone also keeps a little rag. We use it to wipe ourselves after going to the lavatory, then we wash it and put it carefully in our pockets.

The lavatories are a long way from our barrack-hut. With all the dysentery, you sometimes have to run very fast.

A sort of huge wooden table with thirty or forty holes on each side. Everyone sits where they can. In the summer, there are flies everywhere.

The deportees get thinner and thinner and drag themselves more and more often to the lavatories. Then we children roam around the holes, counting those who have hemorrhoids, or those who are so thin that their insides threaten to come out. It's a good game. It passes the time.

The camp fills up so much that there are not enough barrack-huts. They build some on the strip of ground that runs from our barrack-huts to the lavatories.

Among the workers, deportees dressed in rags painted on the back, we find a Frenchman. What a joy! We children go to visit him on the building site in twos and threes, so we won't be noticed by the sentries.

We feel sorry for his red, chapped hands handling the planks and nails. So we beg everyone to give us a little bit of wool or cloth from a piece of clothing, and we make him some sort of fingerless gloves that we bring him in secret.

We learn that he is a common-law criminal. Bah!

We won't be seeing him any more, because we've been spotted.

The camp is full of common-law criminals. Among the *Kapos*, our galley-masters. Always well dressed and well-fed, they replace the Boche who have left for the Front.

Male *kapos*, female *kapos*, with whips in their hands.

Female *kapos* with legs sheathed in fine stockings and soft leather boots. Beautiful girls, often from Germany or Poland. They pass down the central roadway shepherding the herds of prisoners, hurrying them, hitting them.

When they take a dislike to one of them, they hit her until she falls.

Dead bodies lie in every corner. The crematorium chimney smokes all the time.

The smell of Bergen-Belsen, which surprised us at first, no longer bothers us.

A smell of burning flesh, rotting flesh.

I'm rotting too. My hands are covered in impetigo. My

fingers, stuck together with scabs, look like they're webbed. I can no longer bend them. Mother feeds me.

The impetigo spreads. My ears are in shreds. Mother pulls off the scabs with some tweezers saved from a parcel.

I scream, my hair is full of it. They cut around it. Please don't shave my head. Oh no! Please don't shave me.

We go to the infirmary. Doctor Alalouf, a Greek, is devoted to his patients.[21] He goes from one to the other, injecting, scraping, cutting, removing, sewing, clipping, repairing, amid the filth, the lice, the pus.

A single remedy, whatever the ailment, a green pomade in industrial quantities, stored in huge basins. They slather it onto all our sores, then wrap them with strips of paper, and send us on our way.

But what's the matter with me? I have to pass water all the time. And it burns, it burns. Every five minutes I run to the end of the camp.

Distressed, unable to find Mother, I spot a puddle in the mud, pull my underpants down and dip my behind in it. That relieves it a little.

One night, a violent noise wakes us. An Anglo-American bombardment.

They light flares all around the camp to ward off the bombs. At each explosion, everyone says "Good, very good." That's what I think in my heart of hearts, but I'm so afraid.

Each blast of the guns, each counter-blast, shakes me to the core.

I cling to Mother, who puts her arms around me, and holds me tighter when she hears the pounding of my heart.

Oh Mother! I wish I could climb back inside you. I want to bury myself in the tiny bed where we both sleep, with the suitcase at the end, so narrow that we wake one another just by turning over. I want to bury myself in this lice-ridden pile of straw. But not hear the airplane engines as they pass over.

The barrack-hut trembles. The windows shatter. I know this uproar represents hope. But I'm panting with fear.

A bomb finds its way into the kitchens. This complicates the food rationing a little. Never mind. But another demolishes the cremating ovens. Good.

In the time it takes to build another oven, the dead bodies pile up. So they dig quicklime graves, into which they toss the bodies.

Dead bodies pass by every day on the central roadway. It's their Champs-Elysées.

A cart goes from enclosure to enclosure looking for cargo.

They pile them up naked in a corner, one on top of the other, like logs. Then they grab them by the arms and legs, and – one, two, three – they toss them into the cart, which is soon overflowing.

The heads, hands, and feet hang from all sides, tangled, twisted, bent.

Every day I watch the cart go by, pulled by barefoot deportees, in their striped uniforms, exhausted, knowing they'll be in it themselves tomorrow.

Hey, I'm sure I saw that face alive yesterday.

How ugly they are, all these corpses. They're all grimacing.

One head sticks up and stares at me with its cold eyes. I smile at it. Greetings, dead ones. See you soon.

When it rains, water runs through all the holes in the roof, and we come back to find our straw mattresses soaked through.

The rations shrink. Oh, the hunger pangs! What torture! My chest caves in and my bones stick out, but my stomach, how it grows and swells.

Little Josette Weill holds up in spite of everything. We always think she's going to die, she's so blonde and transparent. A baby doll for her brother Jean-Jean and me.

"Truquette's" daughter also clings on, for the moment.

Rose-Marie stays as fresh as a daisy. The others wilt more and more. The most physically marked are Madame Per . . . , Madelon, and Mother, who have been held for the longest.

When I look at Mother properly, I feel like she's been switched with someone else.

Sometimes we're convulsed with hysterical laughter: a joke, a play on words whispered behind the guards' backs, which they don't understand; a happy memory; the slightest thing, and we burst out laughing.

The slightest thing and we burst out crying.

Sometimes we come to blows over nothing, or over the soup, and that's all. But the women here aren't fighting for themselves, they're fighting for their children.

We move. We have to change barrack-huts, quickly. Transport our things, the invalids, the babies and . . . our beds. Our heavy, high, three-story beds. We do it in teams of four, five, six to a bed. We struggle and gasp for breath.

Mother says to me: "Something cracked in my back again." An expression of suffering on her face catches me by surprise. So she's unhappy too, just like me?

I so often see her cleaning an infected throat or binding a swelling that I have forgotten her own health. She has pains in her stomach, and has the bright idea of sacrificing her morning juice, twice, and the heat applied to the right place brings her some relief.

We no longer have a table, not even a bench.

I understand quite a few things in German.

Insults hold no secrets for me anymore. Our movements, kitchens, showers, barrack-huts, *kommandos*, are always accompanied by:

Los, los, Schweine Juden!
Schnell, jüdische Kuh!
Raus, Schweinerei!
Zu fünf, Scheisse, Schmutzstück!

(Move, move, Jewish pigs!
Quickly, Jewish cow!
Get out, swine!
In fives, you shits, you garbage!)

I'm hungry, Mother, I'm hungry.

And Jean-Claude who still won't eat, I could bite him.

A Dutch couple feed their baby with perseverance. He's abnormal. He looks ten months old and is twice that age.

The mother crushes the rutabaga as finely as she can, and slips it in her son's mouth, open like a goose's beak. But the baby dribbles and everything runs out. So the father tries in his turn, and the baby dribbles again. Every day the same.

We are given some raw forage beetroot. It's crunchy and makes a change from the rutabaga. Mother mixes the two in little pieces in my billy can.

As we transport the impossibly heavy soup cauldrons, they sometimes tip over. Ah, how the rations are shrinking!

As a result of spitting everything out, the abnormal baby has just died. How tiny he appears next to the other corpses.

Mother, I'm hungry. I tell her every day, to make sure she knows.

The enclosure next door fills up with men. I don't know where they come from. Bergen-Belsen has no specialities. You find every religion and every nationality here.

Every enclosure, every separate camp suffers its own special regime, more or less horrible. Less for us.

More for our neighbors. During all those hours when I wander around between the barrack-huts, I watch their comings and goings. Accompanied by floggings.

I hear them cry out and see them fall.

They say that at night, they have to get undressed, place

their striped uniforms in the middle of the barrack-hut and sleep naked. That way, they don't waste time undressing the dead bodies in the morning. Those who do wake up have to put on the first pair of pants they pick up in front of them. And when you remember how impossible it is to hold back the dysentery!

I walk out of the barrack-hut with Rose-Marie and her son Michel, and on the other side of the barbed wire, right there, four naked corpses, laid out on the ground with their heads against the wall, await their transfer to the oven.

Rose-Marie has a strange reaction. She grabs hold of Michel and turns him round. I look at them in astonishment. Bah! He's three years old. He'll have to get used to it.

Mother, I'm hungrier and hungrier. Coming back from the roll call, where I got quite cold, for winter is approaching fast, I pull at her sleeve. "I'm hungry, do you hear, I'm hungry."

To get to the showers, we use the central roadway, the Lagerstrasse, and we pass in front of all the enclosures, left and right. Women, men, women, men. Everywhere, now, you see tramps dragging themselves around. A little pile of rags on the ground, still just moving. When we pass by again an hour later, the little pile is no longer moving, he's waiting for the cart.

On his way to the showers, a man tries to get into his barrack-hut. But the door is closed. He is unsteady on his feet, the rags hanging from his body, and he clings to the door handle, shakes it and cries like a child, "Oh, oh, oh!" in great sobs, "Open up, open the door," he cries in a voice drenched with tears," Let me in, Mother, Mother, let me in, oh, oh, oh!" and he cries and cries.

I am so haunted by the image of this man who cries like me when I fall, that I jump when the S.S. guard touches me with his truncheon at the entrance to the showers. Yet it's not the first time.

On the way back, the man is no longer there.

At other times, women who have fallen to the ground hang onto us and murmur words that I don't understand.

Oh lord! Soon, there will be as many people dying on the ground here as there were worms in the camp at Poitiers.

Apparently they almost never feed the men in the camp next door and last night, they ate one of their dead. My friends say it's true.
     The cold. The winter is coming fast. With the snow.

The rations get smaller.

In the center of the barrack-hut, a large stove roars. We jostle to lay the handkerchief or the underwear we have just washed on it. Everyone wants a little corner to dry her worn nightshirt, washed without soap powder, in freezing water, so freezing you have to break the ice to get to it.

We move. To one of the newly constructed barrack-huts. We have to transport the beds, which get heavier and heavier!

While we wait for the new barrack-hut to be installed, we children gather round the stove.

The S.S. chief comes in and sees us. He flies into a rage, orders us to get out and raises his riding crop. Alas, I don't move quickly enough, I lag behind and his riding crop descends on me. Oh! Will I ever forget the burning pain on my back? I clench my teeth and go to hide in the snow, rolling myself in it, crying, choking with pain, mad rage, humiliation, who knows?

Oh! Mother, Mother, why?

During the move, Mother finds a sort of yellow enamel saucepan in the snow. Oh joy. A real treasure, this saucepan.

First of all, we can now go to the lavatory in it at night. We're woken several times every night by the need to relieve ourselves, because of our swollen intestines, a need that obliges us not to go out, since it's forbidden, but to go to a corner of the barrack-hut reserved for this use, which is always overflowing.

Then, we can use it as a bowl to wash in every morning.

And finally, if we want to save a little soup for the evening . . .

Washing. Mother makes me wash every morning. I scream,

the freezing water hurts me so much. But Mother is uncompromising. It's the only thing to keep body . . . and soul together, she says.

I don't want to wash, it hurts too much. You just want to make me wash to make my life miserable. Leave me alone. And anyway, I'm hungry!

Two women sit waiting in the middle of the barrack-hut. An older and a younger one. Mother and daughter. It looks like they're going to die there, right in front of us.

TO DIE OF FILTH.

For it's true, they stare vacantly and they're being eaten up by lice!

From as far away as possible, with arms stretched out, on the tips of their toes, bodies tense, some of the women strip and wash them, then give them some clothes we had collected among ourselves. Then they shave their heads, but it proves impossible. Their scalps are hidden beneath a thick crust of rotten hair, filth, and lice larvae. They scratch and snip, to remove as much of it as possible.

Yes, they had dropped out, these poor women, given in, capitulated, abandoned themselves, let go, abdicated, given up the ghost.

You have to have the will to survive, and not everyone has it.

I watch the lifesaving operation, an avid spectator, fascinated by the quality of the performance, and then I look at Mother out of the corner of my eye, Mother whom

I would gladly beat every morning, with her damned washing for the body . . . and the soul.

(Eventually, the girl will get through. The mother, who was not yet forty, dies exhausted not long after.)

Snow everywhere, thick snow, white snow that muffles the cries, the tears, our lives.

We have to dig paths in the snow. Lift our heavy, swollen legs in the snow. Fall in the snow.

Who could have made me believe that I would ever not want a snowball fight, or a snowman?

Roll calls, horrible, long roll calls in the burning sun. Roll calls in the snow are worse. One hour, two hours, three hours, or more, without moving, on an empty stomach, beneath a leaden sky, with the snow that piles up and seems higher every day. A cold that creeps up from our hands and feet, and down from our heads, a cold that permeates everything, paralyzes, ossifies, petrifies.

A cold that tortures the body and atrophies the mind.

No moving as long as the numbers don't tally exactly.

No touching those who fall.

Stand to attention, the S.S. officer passes by again.

– *Ein, zwei, drei, vier, fünf.*
– *Ein, zwei, drei, vier, fünf.*
– *Ein, zwei, drei, vier, fünf.*

I can't take it any more, Mother. I'm cold, I'm hungry, I'm hurting. I feel my fingers and nose becoming detached from my body. I'm your daughter, do something. You're no longer my mother, you do nothing for me, I don't love you any more, do you hear, I'm cold.

No touching those who fall. Mother is there, lying in front of me, her feet and hands and head covered in snow. A snowflake on her pinched nose, her mouth grey. Mother, Mother, I love you, Mother, open your eyes, Mother, promise me you aren't going to die.

I have to wait until the end of the roll call, almost an hour, to be allowed to touch her.

Oh! How beautiful her eyes are when she opens them!

When we return to the relative warmth of the barrack-hut, after the agonizing cold outside, terrible pains run through our arms and legs. Horrible cramps stiffen our arms. I feel like my toes are going to drop off. Do I still have any blood left in them? I hit my feet as hard as I can, clenching my fists, so that the pain of the blow wipes out that of the cold. It makes me cry, it makes me wince. Sometimes, I suck my big toes to warm them a little. But I think it's actually my mouth that gets colder.

The rations are getting smaller and smaller. They even say that the German troops billeted in the barrack-huts at the entrance to the camp are seeing their meals shrinking. They also say that they only have one real meal a day and, in the evening, some bread with just a scrap of something on it!

Oh! Please give me even just that scrap of something!

In the depths of her pocket, Mother always has an old hair grip, and when she can catch one of us, she automatically cleans out our ears. Her obsession: keeping the children clean.

I start having quite violent pains in my stomach, on the right hand side. Several days in a row. I finally tell Mother.

We file to the infirmary where I am sickened to discover anew the basins of pomade, the paper strips, the pustules and wounds of every kind, the living dead in every corner.

Alalouf, the Greek doctor, examines me and tells me categorically that I'm having an attack of appendicitis.

"I would be more than willing to operate, but as it's not a very violent attack, if you can hold out, let's try to wait for the Liberation. You've seen my set-up and my instruments! . . ."

Obviously, this makes me think there's a big risk that I might not make it through the operation. And even if I don't die in his hands, how would I recover? With injections of rutabaga.

Seeing the operation room has soothed my pain. After all, Father has had chronic appendicitis for twenty years, and Gustave Worms has never wanted to operate on him, saying jokingly: "When your head aches, you don't cut it off."

So I'll wait for the Liberation.

By the way, is there any such thing as a Liberation?

And yet this awful hospital witnesses one very joyful event. Madame S . . . , one night, gives birth to a pretty little baby girl. Mother goes to see her, taking the new mother a piece of chocolate, which she was saving "for even harder times."[22]

I'm all excited. Not so long ago I thought I'd been born in a cauliflower. Cabbages for the boys, roses for the girls and cauliflowers for tomboys like me, and now camps for Jewish babies. How logical it all is.

Mother, whose return from the infirmary I await impatiently to ask, "Were you there, did you see the baby come out?" replies with this sibylline phrase: "I arrived just as the baby broke free."

Broke free! My mother's really losing it. The baby broke free and the hole in my stomach!

Snow. Cold. Hunger. Exhaustion.

Astonished, I observe my legs, which swell up more and more, become red and chapped. And my stomach which balloons. And yet day after day, the diarrhea empties it! And the more it runs, the more I blow up. My shoulders get narrower, but my back stays straight. Strengthened by what Mother told me on the day I wore my star for the first time, I will not bend my spine.
  A star can shine so prettily; mine is like lead.

It's very odd: *my* sores explode like bubbles and disappear. Mother's develop slowly, they open up and start to run, then they take on the unpleasant appearance of rotten meat and make her suffer cruelly. Hands, legs, a veritable breeding ground!

A violent fever strikes down deportees in all the enclosures, and finally infiltrates our barrack-hut.

The first one affected is a beautiful, healthy young woman. Her temperature rises to nearly 41° Celsius. We watch her anxiously, burning and delirious. She rants and raves, thrashing constantly.

The rumor spreads that this fever is called TYPHUS!!

And the rumor proves to be right. Typhus descends upon us. That horrible disease, completely unknown to us all. A temperature of 41° or more, delirium close to madness, and then temporary, and sometimes permanent, blindness and deafness.

Carried by our body lice, those infamous swastika-bearing Boche lice.

And yet, we delouse ourselves every morning. Whatever happens, whatever the weather, we inspect all our clothing, article by article. The lice lodge especially in the seams, in the bottom of pockets, in dark corners, in tight bunches or long strips.

And squish, squish, between the two thumbnails, we crush them. Only thirty today, compared with fifty yesterday!

And that one which just got away, I have to catch it. Ah! The little bastard, cries my neighbor, he jumped onto me.

It's their bites that give us this inhuman fever.

The head-lice have to be killed too. My hair that they cut as soon as it grows back! Overrun with incrusted lice eggs, squish, squish, squish, between the two thumbnails too.

I've seen so many shaved heads over the years that I dream of long hair. When I feel the scissors in mine, I'm terrified at the idea of being shaved. I think it becomes an obsession.

The typhus is gaining on us. An epidemic.[23]

The beautiful young woman dies. The first of our privileged group.

With a tape measure, we cut the bread for everyone. Two centimeters per person per week.

Yvan, our Yugoslavian friend, so young and kind, comes through the typhus with an eye missing!

At the wash basins, kind of metal troughs where the water runs in tiny, tiny trickles, or stops, or freezes, we wash ourselves under the watch of the S.S. guards.

Mother is rinsing the precious saucepan when a Dutch deportee throws himself at her and tries to snatch it. They each pull with all their might, oblivious of their actions, oblivious to one another. His wife arrives, she speaks a little English. So does Mother. They talk. They had lost this saucepan and want it back. It's theirs and they need it.

Mother believes that it maybe saves my life, every night, with my constant diarrhea.

Survive. Weigh up the pros and cons, decide what's best or least bad . . . Think. The most absurd object, the tiniest decision, weighs and weighs heavily, in our world apart.
    Mother decides. She still has a few lumps of sugar. These people have children. Think, survive . . .

They accept the sugar and we keep the saucepan.

The sore that has been plaguing Mother's leg for so long gets deeper every day. Now you can see the bone, all white.

As the Russians advance, the Germans empty some of the camps situated on their path.

Thousands of deportees take the road from Auschwitz to Bergen-Belsen. On foot. The most exhausted ones fall; they shoot them.

And this is how the enclosure next to ours suddenly fills up with human beings whom they say were once women.

A rumor goes round that there are some French women who used to be with us at Drancy, Beaune, and Pithiviers.

We rush over.

I see them . . . thin, haggard, with shaved heads or almost, clothed in striped prisoners uniforms, numbers tattooed on their arms, their feet bare in wooden clogs.

Fania Perla is there, the radiant Fania with her thick brown plait, who made us dance. She has two centimeters of hair, grey hair!

We ask questions. We want to know. Through the wire fence, questions and answers overlap, collide, and run into one another.

– And the Haïm sisters?

– Dead, all three of them.

– And the Baurs?[24]

– Dead.

– And the Daniels?

– Dead.

And him and her and them? Dead, all dead.

– And Jeannine G . . . ?

– She died at the infirmary. As a human guinea-pig. (I remember her very well, she was twenty when she left France.)

– And Guy? I say shyly.

– Up in smoke. Literally.

I scream:

   – Up in smoke, literally? You mean they burnt him?

– Yes, all the children are burnt.

Oh Guy, those beautiful blue eyes with their black eye-lashes, exploding in the flames . . .

I'm cold, I'm hungry, I have dysentery, I have cystitis,
I have impetigo, I'm frightened, I was hit on the back
with a riding crop. One blow, it's laughable. But of
course, I'm privileged. Dear God, why am I privileged and
not Guy?
   I thought I had known the depths of horror, but I was
wrong.

You're somber, Mother. You're thinking about all those
people you helped in the departure staircase, those babies you changed and fed. Those old people you warmed
with a hot water bottle, or a tender word.

And you have just found out that after a terrible journey
in a sealed cattle-wagon, those who had not died during
the journey were killed two hours later.

I know you so well that I know you're thinking "I still
didn't do enough. So that before the gas chamber, the
fire, the quicklime, the petrol injection, the torture, or

who knows what else, they thought of all the love I gave them."

Oh Mother, I who sleep next to you every night, I know you did what you could.

Mother recognized a young Viennese girl with whom she had chatted at Drancy. She lifts her skirt to show us the skeleton-like state of her legs and thighs.

"But you have no underwear!"

Alas, no, in this terrible cold, they have no underwear beneath their prisoners' uniforms. We go to get ours and, those who have them, some socks or a scarf, a sweater, and we throw whatever we can find over the wire fence. Especially since they sleep in canvas barracks.

A miracle! One of our group, a woman of Polish descent, recognizes her sister through the barbed wire! Her sister, who escaped from a ghetto that everyone talks about, and whom she hadn't seen for many years.

Oh! Those poor Polish women, when I think that we felt sorry for ourselves. In France, apart from a few monsters like those you find anywhere in the world, we had quite a lot of people who helped us, saved us. Many people, priests first and foremost, hid the persecuted Jews, sometimes at the risk of their own lives. In Poland, when a Jew managed to escape, the whole village, priests first and foremost, took them to the Germans.

I always get angry with these Eastern European Jews, I resent them for giving me a bad name, because they never integrated, because they were Jews before everything else. But I'm a little ashamed, deep down. How could they integrate? Nobody ever wanted them. They do nothing for the country where they live. They have no country. Yes, that's it, they are stateless. And we must give them a country.[25]

As for me, I have a country. They can do whatever they like to me, say whatever they like, I am French.

And if I do not die here, I know that I will go back home to my country, and will once more park my bottom on the same school benches as my Catholic and Protestant friends, because I am not a Jew living in France, but a French girl of Jewish faith.

The Auschwitz chief, Krammer, becomes our camp chief. Our regime changes too.

With this typhus that is gaining ground, we are overrun with corpses. People are dying everywhere, inside, outside.

The incineration ovens are working full time, the high chimney smokes constantly. The smell of burnt and rotten flesh spreads from enclosure to enclosure.

Enormous holes are dug and they throw in the bodies that cannot be burnt. They call them mass graves.

Day after day in the Lagerstrasse I watch the cart that transports the dead bodies pass by. It passes more and more often. Flop! From the top of the pyramid, a body just toppled over. With a dull thud onto the ground. Two deportees approach to pick it up and put it back in the cart. But they seem exhausted, and in spite of the emaciated state of the corpse, it is too heavy for them. They're not going quickly enough. The *kapo* approaches, shouts, and beats them with his truncheon to hurry them. One of the deportees falls. The *kapo* catches him by the arm and attaches him to the cart.

Oh no! They're not going to put him in there, not while he's still alive! Oh no! I can't watch this. I run to the toilets and while the dysentery bends me double, I realize that this is the first time for months that a horrific scene from camp life has affected me.

So, that means the Boche haven't won! And I start to laugh, also because my neighbor at the next hole, while she relieves herself, is also delousing herself. Two jobs at the same time. That's pretty good!

Since our last move, Mother has been assistant barrack chief, under the orders of Madame Sonnenberg, a German woman. I hate her. The fact that she is Jewish makes no difference, she is German first and foremost. Her father fought in 1914 against my grandfather, and, whatever Hitler thinks, I have nothing in common with her, even if she is Jewish. She barks.

The only Germans with any merit in my eyes are a distinguished elderly couple, who remind me of my grandparents. But they both die.

The typhus hits everywhere. Pierre the journalist, whom I like so much, dies. (A passionate story-teller, and autograph collector, he hung onto Field Marshall Foch's horse to get his, and Foch laughed long and hard at this smart little boy.)

But the chief of the *kapos*, a horrible common-law prisoner, who hits and insults us, also dies.

Ha ha! That gives me some respite.

A Dutch woman breaks our thermometer. What a catastrophe. Only Madame X . . . , has another one. Mother borrows it for an invalid . . . who breaks it.

And Mother, always good, offers to give up her bread for a week to pay for the thermometer. And her offer is accepted!

I have rarely seen Mother so angry. But I never told her so often that I was hungry.

Since this morning, truly, my stomach cramps torment me too much.

I'm hungry, Mother, I'm hungry. Yes, you can look at me oddly, I blame you, I blame you for my hunger.

I feel more and more like I'm living in a whirlwind, a sort of merry-go-round spinning faster and faster. And as it gathers speed, bits fly off, first the smallest, then the biggest, breaking and scattering in every direction.

And I believe that more confusion reigns every minute.

A thousand contradictory statements circulate every day.

They talk of our departure. Then they stop talking about it. But other deportees arrive.

They talk of troops, of guns, of invisible battles.

The S.S. are more and more brutal; the *kapos* scream and hit more and more; more and more deportees die; I'm more and more hungry.

Roll calls, *kommandos*, delousings, soups, dysenteries
   Roll calls, *kommandos*, delousings, soups, dysenteries
   Transport the dead bodies, and hurry!

The rotting of both this unreal situation of ours and of the dead bodies in every corner. The rotting of my morale. I know I am going to die, of lice and hunger.

And if I die, will I find my torturers in the after life?

We little girls play mean tricks on one another. We take one another for a ride, Arlette Volant, Monique Néamat, and I.

With my red-headed pal, we have great discussions, not just playing around, but real discussions. He tells me that they are waiting for us in Jerusalem, in our ancestors' land. But you're Jewish. I've only been Jewish since Hitler. If you go there one day, I'll write to you, really. How could I ever forget you, after what we've been through together! . . .

With the chubby Lévy, I talk about Alsace. He's just arrived from there with his mother, one of the last women to be arrested among us, a hefty peasant, who maintains her air of good health.

And then, they whisper that the oldest of the B . . . s still hasn't started her periods! Because of all the rubbish the Germans put in the soup.

The typhus rages. It seems clear that the strongest, those most recently captured, fall prey more quickly and more easily than veterans like myself.

No doubt after all this time our bodies have got used to the worst attacks. We resist better. We are being extinguished little by little, and I anxiously watch over my tiny flickering flame, my fragile young life.

The more lice I kill, the less they'll bite me. And squish, squish!

I ask whether Guy was burnt before or after his mother, or even right in front of her . . .

Fortunately, via the *kommandos* who work on the Army's boots, I don't know how, but I think by giving our bread rations for several days in exchange, we obtained these German boot bottoms, and some slippers made of the *Wehrmacht*'s uniform material.

The two together, although terribly heavy for our weak legs, at least prevent our feet from freezing.

But my legs, what huge pillars! Marble pillars. I smile at my own joke!

Right! An anti-typhus vaccination, mooted in view of

the scale of the epidemic, which is catching up with the troops.

The medical service is to pass through the barrack-huts. Three doses in one, injected directly into the breast.

The first one to go through it screams for five minutes, beating her chest.

The doctor carrying out the injections takes all these poor thin breasts, slack, distended, wrinkled, between two big fingers and wham! In one fell swoop he sticks in the needle of the big ten centimeter syringe.

Same reaction every time.

Mother, who sees my face, says to me: "Do you want me to take you on my knees and hold you?"

No, I'll go on my own, like a big girl.

I stick out my bare chest and wham, pulling the skin tight, all the liquid goes in.

I am struck rigid, I stop moving, and suddenly, horrible, this tearing pain, there, on the left. What's happening to me? I'm being ripped apart, taken to pieces.

I throw myself onto my mattress, I roll there convulsively, I twist and turn, I think I even drool.

(Rumor has it that the vaccine was supplemented with I don't know what chemical, which explains our pain and the ensuing lack of efficacity.)

Bei mir bist du schein
Veut dire en amour
Que vous êtes plus belle que le jour.
(Popular refrain, half Yiddish, half French.)

Friends teach me several of them, and among others, a beautiful melody whose words I don't know.[26]

Rumors are going round that we are to be exchanged for some German prisoners of war, by the Swiss. "Ah!" says Mother. "If I get through this, I'll go every week to their beauty clinics."

My first meal as a free woman will be a good milky cup of coffee and some croissants, say several of us.

We return to our fine restaurants that evening and I discover *pâté en croûte*. What's more, I own a dog-eared little notebook in which I note a few recipes, among others those for soft and hard caramels.

Please let them hurry. The woman who told me about the *pâté en croûte* will never eat it again.

I'm so hungry, Mother, I can't take it any more.

But you know, I never forget my idea about going on the stage.

"Now, my darling, I have to talk to you seriously. A few of

our companions have given their wedding rings to the *kapos* to get more soup. Do you mind if I wait, if I wait a little bit longer. It's the only thing connecting me with Father. Perhaps we'll be released before it's necessary. Is that all right?"

Mother's wedding ring. Father-Mother, the two who make one . . .

We are the only deportees, the privileged few, who keep their wedding rings!

You know, Mother, I think we should wait a bit longer before we swap it.

How curious: ever since our arrest, from time to time we receive letters from Father. Correspondence from prison to prison.

Apart from the first time, we have to write our letters in German, which presents big problems, because there's a difference between vaguely speaking a language and writing it. . . . And finding a translator at the right time . . . Mother rages with each letter.

Even more astonishing, the parcels, which Father and his comrades sent their wives and children, taking things from their own parcels and paying their guards.

We received three (out of how many sent?), distributed by a Russian deportee from a neighboring enclosure, a nephew of Trotsky's. Gutted parcels, half emptied by the *Wehrmacht*, but of which the little that remained, cigarettes, for example, served as precious currency to obtain more soup from a *kapo*.

And suddenly, I remember the day when I asked the rabbi if God knew about our fate. I tell the oldest B. . . . She replies:

"You know, the Good Lord is the same for everyone . . . But my best friend, at school, told me that her father, in the Militia, shouted Death to the Jews and never misses Mass on Sundays. So I'm going to tell you what I think: there are as many Good Lords as armies in the world, since all the armies pray to the Good Lord before attacking one another! . . ."

Our clothes wear out more and more. Just as we do. Mother and I are wearing pants that have become totally shapeless, sent to Beaune-la-Rolande by Uncle Daniel. Madelon is still hanging on to her everlasting green ski outfit, trimmed with leather, a souvenir of the good old days, before it was gilded with this star that, even at Bergen-Belsen, we must brandish incessantly.

They have filled the camp so much: no more water, we have no more water. Our hands are clammy, our mouths dry . . . Finally, a green truck. We are given two cups per person, for twenty-four hours, drinking and washing included.

Still this feeling of being in a whirlwind, a tornado, an unceasing movement that I cannot resist.

There are no more roll calls!

A rumor circulates that the British are approaching. We hear the guns.

It seems that it is 1945. So then, this summer, I'll be

twelve, and the Allies landed a year ago! Am I going to think, deliberate? About what? About hanging on, if there's a chance of getting through, a chance that gets smaller every day.

And the exchange through the Swiss, . . . and the trucks that, apparently, are waiting for us at the border?

Nothing is true. What's true is the hunger and the lice.

The funny papers that emerge from Mother's pockets and that they call *ausweiss*, allow her, as barrack chief, to cross certain barbed wire fences.

For all that, she doesn't bring back any better news, nor any more soup.

How many deaths per minute, here?

The hunger pangs are really excruciating. If I can manage to sleep on this dung heap of a straw mattress, I can forget them.

Our straw no longer holds together very well on the floorboards, for we burn the planks as we need them, either in the stove or outside, small fires on which we heat our soup or warm up a little water, keeping well hidden from our guards.

I sleep in my dirty cubbyhole. It suits the animal that I've become.

And that night, up you get, walk, quickly, *raus*, to the showers!

We cross the camp, in the semi-darkness, scarcely coun-
tered by a few meager light bulbs. Cries, complaints.
In disjointed ranks, our column drags its feet, mothers
holding their children tightly, for we have understood! Oh
the gut-wrenching fear! So it's tonight, our big event, the
return to Eternity. But why at night?

All along the Lagerstrasse, I make out the enclosures,
one after the other, the grey barrack-huts against the
pine trees, the naked corpses piled up like logs, sentinels
outlined in the distance. A dog barks, a man shouts, a
kapo gives an order, an S.S. guard sniggers.

I've never seen a concentration camp at night. What a
nightmare. I try to count the barbed wire gateways, six
more, then five, and then four, and then they're going to
kill me. And how are they going to kill me?

We march in silence. My hand in Mother's, the clip clop
of our clogs on the stones of the path. Patches of night
mist that I take for ghosts.

My heart beats fast, my heart beats terribly fast, because
it knows it's going to stop. Wham! They're going to still
the pendulum of my twelve year old clock.
   A miracle, it's a real shower. A night shower. What were
they thinking of? The return to the enclosure seems
glorious. My ghosts have turned into angels. Clean, deloused, alive.

This time it's real, we're leaving. In a kind of seething
mob, an uproar, a coming and going in every direction.
Deportees arrive from every camp in Germany. They sort
them into groups, or if necessary, burn them here, and
we're leaving!

And quickly, *raus*, with no baggage, no possessions, just the little bundle of the Wandering Jew.

Trucks line up in front of the wire fences.

There is talk of Theresienstadt, a camp in Bohemia, where Léon Blum and other well-known people are held.

We are to be accompanied by the Greeks, the Dutch,[27] and the Albanians.

In short, all the hostages whom the Germans drag in their wake.

Squatting on the ground, in a corner, we greedily gulp down a handful of rice, cooked hurriedly on a fire made with floorboards. The rice we had been keeping for even harder times.

We empty our package. All the treasures we'd saved in spite of the successive moves, the little rag, a souvenir of a dead friend, a photo from the time when we were free. Even Father's two books, his two first and still only books. Mother, I can't leave those, we have to take them. So Mother tears off the two covers, including the one of Dona Conception, drawn by Father himself, and thrusts them into her pocket. We also take the lucky knife.

People are running in all directions, among the noise, the orders, the counter-orders.

We shout goodbye to the deportees next door, and to the dying as well.

In the general panic, in the scuffle of the departure, with gates opening and closing, huge soup containers passing by, *kapos* shouting at the top of their voices, packages, bundles, bits of clothing scattered here and there, our Polish companion, the one who recognized her sister among the arrivals from Auschwitz, manages, I don't know how, to get her in with us. Quickly, she takes off her prisoner's uniform, and we all chip in to clothe her.

A German shouts that the fittest will leave on foot. So Mother drags me toward the trucks. Everyone is trying to haul themselves up. We fight. The S.S. beat us with their truncheons. Mother and I manage to climb up and the truck sets off, then suddenly stops: The deportees from the next block have joined us to try and escape.

The S.S. drag them down and shoot them. I look at the twelve dead bodies and we leave for Bergen station.

A train is waiting for us, made up of fourth class carriages, cattle wagons, and simple roofless platforms.

Next to the tracks, an enormous pile of rutabagas and another of forage beetroot. We rush to take some. The S.S. shoot. An Albanian collapses.

Mother and I are lucky enough to find room in the fourth class carriage. We pile in, we squeeze up, men, women, children of all nationalities. All our fellow-travelers exhale a fetid smell. We sit on benches, running the length of the carriage, or on the ground. Lice swarm on the partitions and jump onto us (we learn later that this train had been used to transport people with typhus).

We move on. We travel for whole days at a time. Then we stop for hours. And we start off again. We change tracks. We stop again.

We quickly use up the bread and margarine given out on the first day. And the rutabagas snatched at the station. Then they stop giving us anything at all.

At the stops, our guards allow us to pick the nettles along the tracks. We cook them on two stones. To drink, we take water from the ditches.

We are overrun with lice. We squash more than fifty a day. At the stops, we all get out onto the track, strip off completely, men, women, children, and delouse ourselves like monkeys at the zoo. The battle against the typhus-carrying lice.

When a fellow-traveler dies while the train is rolling, we throw the body out of the window.

A few men try to escape. I ask myself where they could possibly go.

The train rolls on and on, like a mad train. We go back through villages we already crossed the day before.

After a town called Lüneberg, the S.S. taunt us by telling

us that we were almost rescued, since the British had just arrived there.

That night, the Dutch woman in front of us goes crazy. She tries to strangle her child. Her husband ties back her hands with his belt. Then she dies and we abandon her on the tracks.

The British, then Russian planes take our train for a German troop carrier. They machine-gun us. Now we have dead and injured, especially in the roofless carriage.

Once, the S.S. guards allow us to take some potatoes from a field. Wolves. We have become wolves. We fight against the Albanians, the Greeks, the Dutch.

Apart from that time, we eat only nettles. So dysentery bends us double. We wade in it. Our feet, our legs. We stink. And we scratch ourselves until we bleed.

More and more dead. More and more mad people!

A prolonged stop. Mother heads across the fields, like other fellow-travelers, to try and find a little food. She doesn't come back. I search for her, I run everywhere, I ask everyone for information, the S.S. blow the whistle for the departure, and I can no longer leave the train because they'll shoot at me. The train starts up and Mother still isn't back. Never, since 26 July 1942, have I known such agonizing worry. Where is Mother? The train rolls on and I am alone. My heart is pounding, my head is bursting. Mother, it's not possible. I slip in the liquid shit that covers the floor, going from one end of the wagon to another, hoping to glimpse I don't know what. Mother, it's not possible. My temples pound. My hands are clammy. You can all die, all of you around me, but not Mother, not Mother. I have nothing, nothing, if I don't have Mother![28]

My terror lasts a few hours. At the next stop, Mother climbs back in.

She had fainted with exhaustion, and on coming to had said: "This is it for me, I can't go any further. Go on without me." And our companions managed to drag her and hoist her up into the last carriage as the train shuddered into motion. In front of the laughing armed Germans.

When it rains, we make fires under our carriages. The S.S. stamp them out on the pretext that we'll set everything on fire. So we eat raw nettles.

The train rolls on. We stop, just long enough to wash, if a stream runs close to the tracks, or to pick some nettles, sometimes a few dandelions.

The S.S. pass from time to time in the carriages and distribute a few beatings.

We cross the suburbs of Berlin and witness a bombardment. It raises our hopes a little.

At one stop, one of our companions doesn't get out. When we get back in, he is dead. So we throw him out

of the carriage. As this happens often, I think of Tom
Thumb, who left a trail of stones; we leave a trail of bodies.

Our convoy crosses a road where military trucks are passing by. The Allied planes appear and bombard them. The
train stops, and the S.S. jump out and throw themselves
down in the surrounding fields.

Two of our carriages burn. So we tie everything white
we have left to branches, using them as flagpoles, then
on the roofs, at the windows, the doors, we put shirts,
underpants, rags, so that the Allies will see that, in spite
of the presence of our armed guards, we are not soldiers.

Escape, but escape to where? We don't speak the language, there is fighting everywhere, and we can barely
walk.

The train rolls on. Left, right, east, west. Everywhere
the guns thunder. We are submerged with lice, we are
vanquished. Our stomachs run. We have terrible battles
among ourselves. And madmen, madmen.

During an air raid, our guards throw themselves to the
ground in fear, and some Greeks take advantage of this to
break into the carriage containing the military supplies.
We all fight, but we're weaker than these men driven wild
by too much deprivation, and when we get to the booty,
all that's left is packets of soap powder!

We are all crazy. A Dutchman beats Mother black and
blue because she asks him not to crush me as he sleeps.
    She lies panting on the ground.

Let him crush me. What does it matter. The guns pound. But will they come quickly enough?

I'm not even hungry any more.

My hair is stuck together, matted with lice eggs. My pants are stiff with diarrhea and split at the knees. I smell of rotting flesh.

A stranger coming upon us would think he was hallucinating, with our stinking carriages covered in excrement, the floors strewn with comatose invalids and bleeding gunfire victims. With our nettle gruel, full of dirt, fought over by stumbling phantoms. With the dead bodies we leave in our wake.

From time to time I want to scream, but it would be a waste of my energy.

Berlin is burning. All around us we hear the noise of fighting. We roll on. "We're coming to our destination" say our guards.

Their numbers, what's more, are shrinking. The S.S. officer disappears.

The destination, we learn after our rescue, is a mined bridge, on the Elbe river, where our train was supposed to blow up.

We no longer hear the guns. The train has stopped moving. Everyone's asleep. The track follows a road.

Early next morning, the noise of cars and horses wakes us: officers on horseback, soldiers in khaki shirts,[29] the Russians, the RUUUSSSIAAANS! What a cry!

A few deportees die of joy.

I kiss so many people . . .

And then, I see them go by, my guards, with their hands in the air.

The fittest among us run toward the nearest village.

"Not you, Mother, I still shudder at the thought of your disappearance in the train. What if you fell, or a hidden gunman shot you down?"
    "No, no, I'll survive. And we still have to eat."

The Russians help them to break down the doors of some rabbit hutches and chicken-sheds. A soldier smiles at Mother, she points to her mouth to say, "I'm hungry," and he takes an egg out of his pocket!
    Poor little Russian soldier, how many horrors you must have seen, in the war, and how deprived you must be of

the company of women, to make advances to my poor wreck of a mother!

Back at the train, we devour our booty. Sugar by the spoonful, pâté, jam, bacon. We mix everything. Mother wrings a chicken's neck!

One of our companions skins a rabbit in one fell swoop, like taking off a dress. We swallow, straight from the tubes, condensed milk taken from a nearby factory, tubes that don't yet have their caps. Everything goes in.

There is such a thing as a full stomach, then!

The Russians tell us to go and find somewhere to stay in the village. We walk there.

Deserted by its inhabitants, by the women especially (for fear of the Russian soldiers! . . .)

It is called Tröbitz.

Nana precedes us into a house at the end of the village, at the top of the street.

What a fine thing a house is, so cosy and welcoming. I visit everything. The living room with its flowered curtains. The dining room with its polished wooden floor. The kitchen with its earthenware stove.

And the provisions! All these full jars! Can it be possible, so many things to eat!

So *they* eat during wars. And they drink, sometimes a hundred meters from where they burn people. They must hear the cries, mustn't they?

Photos of Hitler, even between the piles of sheets, in the cupboard.

I wash myself, *I wash myself all over. I wash with hot water.*

I actually think I have no more lice.

The villagers return from the forest where they had gone to hide when the Russians arrived They come in and greet us, almost on their knees, they should be ashamed! What obsequiousness! What servility in their looks, in their words. They are prostrate. *I* have never crawled.

I taste the cherries in the garden, and the radishes. The two at the same time make peppery cherries, how delicious!

The next morning, the cherries and the radishes are torn up. The Boche took everything during the night.

I still have lice.

I've been released, yes, but the war isn't over. They're still fighting near here. I've been released, but I could still die.

Josette Weill, our baby saved so many times, our blonde baby whose porridge I used to finish at Drancy, Josette died last night.

Liberated on 23 April, I know the date, and dead on the twenty-fourth. Jean-Jean, her brother, and Odette her mother, take her to the German cemetery in the village. Oh Odette! How will you go on living now?

And then Jean-Lévy, my friend from Alsace, we meet him in the road. He is pushing a wheelbarrow, and in the wheelbarrow is his mother, his dead mother, whom he's taking to the cemetery up ahead, alone.

Oh, my Liberation, how brilliant I imagined you!

No, the war is not over. Our Russian liberators remind us of that by closing the doors and shutters for the night. No light must filter through. The Germans are still shooting.

All night, the shock troops move up toward the front, with a terrifying noise of engines, chains, and moving vehicles. Shock troops cannot be beautiful in any country in the world.

Several women are molested, one of our companions is even raped in front of her son!

Those of our companions who come from Russia have warned us not to say we are Jewish, the Russians are traditionally anti-Semitic. And in fact, one of the first questions asked by our liberators, wanting to know the reason for our presence here is: "Are you Jewish?" We are evasive. French, we reply. Ah!

As Nana speaks Russian, several officers come into the house to chat. They give us mixtures of fruit juice and vodka to drink.

We squeeze up, because the officer wants the big room. He sleeps there in the same bed as his orderly, who himself sleeps fully-clothed, with his gun in his arms!

The Russians give us very little to eat because, in truth, they have very little, and they have to feed their troops who are fighting. I learn to say "*rleb*," bread, and "*spassiba*," thank you.

They tell us that deportees often die on the day they are set free, because they eat too much, all at once. Our bodies, unused to the food, cannot withstand the onslaught of such huge quantities.

Oh, my Liberation, how glorious I imagined you!

I have trouble getting rid of my lice. We burn our foul clothing and put on whatever we can find. I dress in an old blouse, which has been darned but is clean, and a skirt in the same state, and I put on a pair of misshapen shoes, black and split, a bit big for me.

Mother slips on a shapeless blue dress, whose flared skirt hangs flatly on her jutting bones, and whose two or three dozen little buttons trickle down her thin spine.[30]

Oh! Mother, Mother, my pretty mother, it's been so long since I looked at you, I could hardly even imagine you in a dress any more, and now I see you, *and I see*. My dearest mother, do you see too, do you know that you no longer look like a woman, do you know you look like an old clown who won't give up?

Oh my Liberation, how happy I imagined you!

And what if Father didn't recognize Mother? And all these

old sores on her skin. What if he were disgusted! And me! With my sticking out stomach and my heavy, blue-tinged legs.

And is Father alive anyway? And where?

Some prisoners of war from a neighboring camp say that the Russians mistreat them. Some have taken their wedding rings by force. The Russians show the deepest scorn for prisoners of war.

Oh my Liberation, how joyful I imagined you!

Mother, lying on a stretcher placed on the ground of the little courtyard, has typhus, and I'm waiting for them to come and get her to take her to the hospital set up by the Russians.

I talk to her, and already she can no longer hear me, for the typhus has made her deaf.

I shuffle from one foot to the other, standing in front of her, and I listen, my eyes filled with tears.

"My darling, so many months, so many years of struggling to come to this. I love you, I love you so much, and tell Father that I love him."

The cart comes to take her. I love you, I love you.

"Oh joyful land," says the deportees' song, "where we can love, love for ever."

By what miracle does this song make the rounds of all the concentration camps?

Oh my Liberation, how full of laughter I imagined you!
  I think the war is finished.

I go on living, I go on living like this, peacefully, in my little German house.

Nana, Madelon, and Jean-Claude have left for Kirchhain, near Torgau, a few kilometers away from the place where the Russians and the Americans met, leaving me in the care of Rose-Marie. I go for walks with Michel, her son.

Nicolas, a young Russian medical officer, recently released, becomes very friendly with us and spends almost every day at our house. He explains that he is already dreading the return to his country: in Russia, you return victorious, or not at all. Shame on all prisoners. (The Russians, what's more, never recognized the Geneva Convention.) Now I understand the behavior of the Russians toward the French prisoners of war, their deep disdain for them and sometimes their mistreatment.

I know that Mother is still alive. We eat potatoes. My teeth hurt. I feel feverish.

Nicolas puts a thermometer under my arm, or in my mouth. I put it somewhere else, as we do in France.

I'm so afraid of having typhus.

From time to time the Germans ask us to settle their disputes. What strange people.

Rose-Marie makes herself a dress out of the flowered curtains from the living room. The German owner notices and scolds her. Rose-Marie, who speaks good German, tells her:

"Do be quiet, Madame. My entire house was ransacked. My husband has been a prisoner for five years, my son and I for three, and my country plunged into suffering, so don't go on about your curtain!"

"Ah! I didn't know all that" she replies weakly.

As for me, I also think about Rose-Marie's arrest, early in the morning, marched right around the town, surrounded by soldiers, and naked under her transparent nightshirt.

The typhus continues its ravages. The survivors come out of the hospital, smiling and thin, their heads shaved.

The Russians put the village into quarantine. No one can leave any more. We might contaminate everyone.

I wonder if anyone believes we even exist any more.

Madame Avram manages to escape!

I learn that during a bout of despair, Mother shouted:

"I don't even remember what my daughter looks like; I can't even picture her face. I've forgotten her, I wouldn't recognize her!" And she cries and cries and cries.

I quickly write her a little letter, which Madame Jacobi

passes on to her, and I attach a little flower picked on the wayside:

"Dearest, darling Mother,

Madame Jacobi has just passed on your message and I'm replying straight away. I am very well, I'm in good health. I have put on lots of weight. I am here alone with Rose-Marie and Michel. Madelon has gone to live in Kirchhain, as has Nana. Rose-Marie looks after me very well. As for everything you asked Madelon for, cakes and anything else, it's impossible, for we have absolutely nothing. I heard that you no longer have a fever. Imagine, what a joy for me! I send you hundreds and thousands of kisses and hope to see you very soon. Your dearest daughter who is thinking of you.

Francine."

My friend Toli's mother, Madame Jacobi, who has become a nurse, says to me one day: "Your mother seems to be a little better; do you want to come and see her?"

An old quarantine block. A makeshift hospital. Through the open window, I can talk to my mother.

I glimpse all these women in their creased, yellowed hospital gowns, with their shaved heads, their feverishly bright eyes; apathetic or agitated.

Mother, Mother!

"Ah, there you are!" cries this specter. "There you are, you little thief; you took my tube of condensed milk, I knew it, thief, thief, thief."

Yes, she's better, I even believe she's out of danger. She can hear, she can see, her temperature has settled at 37–38°, but she's lost her mind.

I slowly set off home, all alone, too young, hanging my head, with my too big shoes that hurt me, in the May sunshine, which we usually love so much.

The Russians, who know about typhus, told us that it does indeed disturb the mind for a few weeks.

And what if it stayed like that? What if it stayed like that? Who would care? In my enclosed village, no one! And the rest of the world? Is there a rest of the world?

The hospital is run by a woman doctor, Commandant Sokoletskaia, with, under her orders, four doctors, captains, of whom only one is a man. They all care for us with exemplary devotion.

These curious Russians, whom they decorate sometimes two, three, or four times with the same distinction, and who wear all four of them on their chests, spread out, ribbon and medal, sometimes every day.

The sun shines. The hospital gets no emptier. The typhus doesn't seem to want to attack me. Mother begins an agitated convalescence. I never see her.

The astonishing discipline of the Russians. When an officer speaks to a soldier, the soldier stands to attention throughout the conversation, with no order to "stand at ease"!

I lead a very calm life, in my imprisoned and contaminated village. The typhus continues to kill, here and there. The Russians take very, very good care of us.

I know how to say lots of things in Russian: *ya-niay-paniaymayou parouski* ("I don't speak Russian," written my way!)

My hair grows back.

We were released almost two months ago now, and I don't think about it much. I go for walks with Michel, I play with my friends. I think about nothing. I go on living.

I go on living and I'm doing the lunchtime washing up when the thunderclap resounds:
    "Francine, your father's here!"[31]

What a jolt in my stomach! I drop everything, I slip on my clogs so I can run faster and then, in the distance, I see two French officers. And then, no one need say any more, I run toward one of them. He tells me later that I haven't seen him for *five years*, but I know it's him and not the other one, and I jump on him, and I hang onto his army jacket, and I laugh, and I cry, and he laughs and he cries. And your mother? In the hospital? How is she? Out of danger? Ah! Madame Avram, who managed to make it to France, told me that she was dying, no, no, but we're not allowed to go to the hospital. Wait, with me you can, and kiss me again, and you too. Oh Father! This is the happiest day of my life![32]

We leave for the hospital. Ten minutes on the main road. We head toward the barracks. Madame Jacobi, our nursing companion, comes with us. A Russian sentry blocks our passage. He aims his rifle at Father!

How can we explain to him? There's nobody around. A Russian nurse appears and sorts everything out.

We go into the ward, and all the shaved heads lift up, astonished.

"You've made a mistake, says Father, backing away, this is the men's ward.

No, we have to shave them because of the typhus."

In Mother's ward, Dora, who is convalescing, but still so feminine, has taken a towel and quickly wrapped it round Mother's head.

Father, this white clown, who is laughing and crying at the same time, it's Mother! They kiss and hug, look at one another, and, in her emotion, the turban falls and Mother appears with her shaved head!

On the road back to the village, Father walks straight forward, looking ahead, rigid, absent, he holds my hand and repeats:

"They shaved her, they shaved her . . ."

Wartime never brings out the beauty in women . . .

The other officer, who succeeded in finding us with Father after so many difficulties, is Pierre Lang, Madelon's husband, Jean-Claude's father, our companions from the early days.

Commandant Sokeletskaia invites Father and Pierre to dinner. I'm allowed to go in for the dessert. What a spectacle!

The meal is served by Cossacks in billowing shirts, slung with cartridges, crowned with hats of black astrakhan with red cuffs and threads of silver. They bend themselves double to present the dishes, ceremoniously, as if we were princes.

Everyone drinks a lot, vodka mixed with Bordeaux! Even Father, who never used to drink so much as a glass of wine.

Everyone is laughing, and when Father realizes that there are thirteen of them at the table, he laughs like a madman!

Father and Pierre leave again, to see General Faminine, head of the military region, to tell him they have found us. For General Faminine was unaware of the presence of French women at Tröbitz, a situation brought to light by Madame Avram's successful escape.

So we were among the lost, the forgotten victims of the war.

Every war has its forgotten people, sometimes missing for a very long time . . .

After everything Father has told me, I ask him what would have become of us, without his stubbornness.

After his camp was liberated, along with his comrades, including Pierre Lang, he finds a German car and heads for Bergen-Belsen: dead bodies, dead bodies rotting everywhere. The British army, who liberated the camp, are awaiting medical reinforcements, devastated by the horrifying discovery they've just made.

Father looks for us everywhere, visits everything, examining everything he passes: syringes for injecting petrol into the heart, exploding pencils that kill those who write with them; he even inspects the mass graves, turning over the bodies, trying to recognize us, supported by a British officer who gives him some whisky to get him through, both of them crying. They drink the whole bottle, but never stumble . . .

No trace of us. Not a single document, not a single dossier. The Germans always burn everything before fleeing . . .

At the end of his strength and courage, in the midst of these acres of Death, he meets a deportee with typhus who vaguely remembers the group of hostages who left around 9 April, for an unknown destination.

So he returns quickly to Lübeck, informs his comrades, (there are ten of them, whose ten wives are together), manages to get repatriated to Paris before the rest of the camp, arrives during the general celebrations, but he has to keep looking.

The Ministries – War, Prisoners, Deportees, Repatriation, nothing, no one has heard of us.

Telegrams to the Anglo-American H.Q., in Sweden, in Switzerland. Nothing.

Appeals on the radio: Lieutenant Robert Christophe is looking for a group, etc., etc.

We have disappeared with the phantom train.

And then one day, Madame Avram arrives: "I ran away from Tröbitz, where our group is, I walked a hundred kilometers, then the Americans took me in and sent me home. Go quickly, everyone is sick! What's more, it's already too late for your wife!"

Quickly, a mission command, given by Commandant de Boissieu, General de Gaulle's future son-in-law; a plane, Pierre and Father avail themselves of one belonging to an officer on a mission, an old canvas plane! France is poor. Three hours to get to Leipzig!

In a Jeep, that most curious contraption, loaned by the Americans, they try every day to get into the Russian zone, and every day, in spite of the precious help of Commandant Rochcau, a French chaplain who speaks Russian, they are sent back, with armed Russian soldiers on their Jeep, to the American zone. They sometimes get as far as twenty-five kilometers in and have to retrace their steps every time.

Twelve days of trying and Madame Avram had told them to be quick!

Finally, one day, a Russian officer takes them to General

Faminine, head of the military region. His fist bangs on the table, he is angry, there is no French group in Tröbitz! Let Father and Pierre go, and if they find nothing, their "situation will be difficult." (We know what that means in 1945 in the Russian zone.)

Quickly, drive along bombed routes, among the carcasses of tanks and burnt trees, so fast that the Jeep turns over in a field. Quickly, cross the villages decorated with red flags (the coat of arms with the swastika decorating the center, just unpicked, has left its mark), quickly . . . and I am reunited with my father!

So Father leaves and comes back again. He goes into action. Contradictory rumors are going round. The Russians don't want to give us back! Then they agree to give back those that the typhus has spared. So I can leave, but not Mother; finally, they let those who have recovered and are no longer contagious leave, and Mother can leave, but not me!

Father takes charge of the convoy of invalids, Pierre of the few people in good health (everything is relative), who will go back by plane. And the others will follow, under the supervision of Commandant de Rochcau, as soon as the Allies have trucks or trains.

It's not up to two Frenchmen, ex-prisoners, to decide . . .

Ambulances wait to drive us to the American zone, where a medical train will take us to Paris. But I'm not entitled to it, I must leave with Pierre, in the "healthy people's" convoy, which will get underway in a few days, or in the convoy of trucks. So, in order not to be separated from

Mother and Father, with whom I've only just been re-united, I'm going to leave in secret, no questions asked, very quickly, do a runner.

Some of the Russians insist that I be disinfected and showered before taking me on board.

"Father, are you sure they're not going to shave my head?" I'm scared to death.

Father lunches with the lady doctor-commandant, he's invited to her mess. (She makes him raise toasts to de Gaulle and Stalin, with more vodka and claret.) In the meantime, I run back to the house and, in a little knot-ted handkerchief, I wrap up all my treasures: the lucky knife, worn from cutting so many bread rations; a silver die, given to me by a deportee who had since died; a propelling pencil given by another deportee as he was leaving; some *Ausweisses*; a steel brooch found on 23 April; the four-leaf clover picked in Pithiviers during the search; a recipe book, disinfected and warped in the process; a few letters from Father; etc.

I go down the main street of Tröbitz, without even looking at it, faking nonchalance, and when Father joins me in the ambulance, looking slightly gray-faced, I wait, sitting on the floor, well hidden between the two women transport officers' seats.

We set off. Mother, behind, lying on a stretcher, Father in front, in the Jeep, which leads the column. Farewell Tröbitz. I don't even take a last look, I'm so afraid of being discovered and sent to the other group. I could never describe Tröbitz, I never looked at it!

Mother moans with every jolt.

The French women ambulance drivers start to pamper me with such generosity that, little by little, my confidence returns. After a few kilometers, I get up, and I observe.

Farewell to the Russians, farewell and thank you. I will never forget. We meet them on the road, they're heading east, we're heading west.

Caravans of cars, trucks, carts, old carriages, ox-carts . . . all loaded to overflowing with furniture, paintings, machines, mattresses. I even see a piano on an old chara-banc, pulled by a mule, driven by a man in a *moujik*'s shirt. Herds of cows, too. All heading east. Bravo, the Russians, take what you can, it's your turn now!

A chicken flutters, and whoosh, a soldier with a fur cap puts it on top of a pile of furniture, and off we go!

What movement, what coming and going. At the cross-roads, women soldiers have taken the place of the police, machine guns on their shoulders, covered in smiles, with little red flags to halt us. They check our papers and look inside the ambulances, with yellow flags in their other hand to let us through, Father in his Jeep and the six ambulances that follow.

I spot an officer with cartridges on his chest, drink-ing and laughing. To your very good health, General Dourakine!

I turn round. Mother, do you know what I'm thinking about? General Dourakine! Mother groans, and the ambulance drivers laugh, but they don't understand. They couldn't understand that, if I'm thinking about General Dourakine, it means I'm really free and that everything inside me has understood that, because before, two months ago, I could only think about eating.

At Torgau, they play the Marseillaise for us, under enormous portraits of Stalin, Roosevelt, Churchill, Truman, Joukov, and de Gaulle, decorated with eight stars on his sleeve! . . .

We arrive in LEIPZIG, which is occupied by the Americans.[33] We drive around amid the ruins. The hospital to which they take us, decapitated of its upper floors, now rises only two stories high amid the rubble.

The American nurses leave the stretchers in the entrance hall, on the ground, one next to the other. I am the only non-invalid, the only child.

Within a few minutes, we find ourselves in an unknown universe: in wonder, I contemplate all the soldiers with their youthful smiles, the cleanliness, the peaceful atmosphere, the organization, and, above all, the kindness bestowed on us, so soothing, so gentle, for our battered hearts.

I'm made a great fuss of. The Russians were efficient, but never once did a Russian officer take me on his knees to give me a sweet.

An officer approaches me: *"Vous êtes juive,"* he says to me in French, you're Jewish.

"Yes."

"So," he replies laughing, with his nasal accent, "we're brothers. Let's shake hands."

In the morning, while the doctors and nurses get busy with the invalids, I'm taken to the first floor, to the canteen. There, another surprise awaits me: everyone takes their own special moulded tray, then passes in front of a sort of bar, choosing from the dishes presented as he goes along.

Delighted, I contemplate my tray loaded with astonishing foods for my breakfast: an egg, some sausages, some pancakes covered with a very sweet sauce, white bread! Butter, jam, milk!

Father and I leave on foot, hand in hand, for a tour of the town, amid the rubble. We get to know one another again.

A few Germans are already clearing the streets.

We are given big labels filled with information to hang on our chests: surname, first names, age, camps, years spent in detention, illnesses . . .

The train home. Prisoners of war of all different nationalities; male deportees; a medical carriage for us. We are joined by a group of babies belonging to French deportees sent to do forced labor. They're being brought back to France to be placed with the Social Services, for no one knows the names of their fathers, taken during the debacle. Almost all born out of wedlock. Pretty as pictures.

One is nicknamed The Priest by their transport officer, because he is apparently the son of a Frenchwoman and a German abbot.

I'd never imagined what a medical train would be like: a hospital on wheels with beds made up with very white sheets, cupboards full of phials and medicines, a bathroom, treatments of every kind, shining toilets, and all these tall American nurses, so healthy, so clean, so full of smiles. (Several are of Chinese descent.)

My presence and that of the babies drives them completely mad with delight. For so many months they have seen nothing but wounded and sick, they never tire of contemplating us, pampering us, and playing with us.

Like many trains coming from Germany, ours is made up of French carriages and locomotives stolen by the Germans and recovered by our troops.

So I'll be traveling in a suburban train marked SNCF!

We wait for hours at Leipzig station before setting off. There are problems caused by tracks half destroyed by the fighting, prisoners and deportees migrating in every direction, refugees from everywhere and nowhere, troops to be transported.

After two or three hours, Mother, at the end of her tether, asks for something to eat, a sudden hunger: cramps. Father looks for something and finds nothing. We don't know where the restaurant car is. On a track opposite a train is waiting, packed with the survivors we see every-where, with no family, no country.

One of them has an apple and gives it to Father.

Father sleeps in another carriage and joins us every time the head doctor allows it, not often enough for his liking. He gazes fondly at Mother, Mother who moans, or tosses and turns, and who rants and raves deliriously.

I beg from the nurses all their half-used packets of ciga-rettes, explaining that they're for my father, and they give them willingly. Which means that every time Father appears, I greet him with a new packet. He explains that it's not right to beg like this, that in normal life, it isn't done, and we're going back to normal life.

Yes, I did say "*rleb, rleb!*" to the Russians, "cigarettes, cigarettes!" to the Americans. I understand that I must no longer do it.

As a result of the fighting, there is almost nothing left of our railway tracks and bridges, the entire French railway network in short, and our train will have to make a big detour to get to France via Limburg, in the south of Hol-land, which will add considerably to our journey, but will allow us to drop off the Dutch and Belgian deportees on the way.

The military destination for this train is Reims. But Fa-ther, as chief of our convoy, hopes to get us transported to Paris all the same. For from Reims we will find nothing to get us to the capital. Everything this country possesses in the way of carriages and trucks must remain available for the troops.

As we roll on, I make my plans: first, do some acting in the theater, because I feel it like a burning need. Then become the first woman president of the Republic!

And what if every Sunday, instead of a religious service, we showed all the heads of state throughout the world the spectacle of a child burning? Maybe they'd think twice about declaring a war . . .

Oh Guy . . .

Germaine Marx, whose bunk is the one before Mother's, has dreadful spots all over her behind. Every few minutes, she throws back her sheets in a gesture of exasperation, and when Father walks into our carriage, he is greeted by this sight.

Poor Germaine, who's totally unaware of this because she's delirious.

When we remember she's the daughter in law of a rabbi, Father and I can't help laughing!

What a journey! I too am delirious, but with ecstasy.

We are fed like princesses, and often with completely unexpected combinations. For example a mixture of tuna fish and peanuts appears one day on our plates. Delicious!

I will always think of Guy every day . . .

The American nurses gently approach Mother to calm her and sing songs to her. She is suffering, I don't know where, and tries to stutter a few words in English to say that she wants some medication. She cries "injection, injection!"

The head doctor looks at Father sadly, tapping his index finger against his temple and saying with his heavy accent, "You wife, lieutenant, he have screw loose!"

I really believe he's right.

Our train goes through Holland; it stops at Maastricht to drop off the Dutch survivors. Then in Belgium at Liège for the survivors from that country.

We are approaching France and my heart beats faster. Father, do you think we're dreaming?

Jeumont. Jeumont-la-France! The station is decked with flags, the crowd on the platform applauds us, blows us kisses, and then the Marseillaise is played over the loud-speakers.

Then Mother comes out of her lethargy, I think she understands, she cries, the others cry too, and through the window the people see these poor shaved heads and skeleton-like faces and start crying too.

What a noise, what a hubbub! But what a wonderful noise, and what a joyful hubbub!

Tears run down my cheeks, I touch Mother, I touch Father, I look at the flags, I smile at this crowd of people who want to approach me. A nurse from the Red Cross gives me an orange. An orange! I ogle it admiringly.

"But you can eat it!"

I can eat it! I smell it first and feel it and show it to Mother, and Mother cries even harder.

And Germaine throws off her sheets, and we have to cover her. And I laugh. And everyone laughs.

The train moves off again slowly, between the decked platforms and the waving hands.

Oh my country, my native land, here you are. I found the little bits of Holland and Belgium that I glimpsed on the journey beautiful, but you are even more beautiful.

Of course the grass is greener, the breeze sweeter, and the sun brighter.

I squash my nose against the window, and devour with my eyes what I thought I'd never see again.

The American doctor comes up to me and murmurs in my

ear, in his best French: "You know, your country, it's the most beautiful one!"

We're approaching Paris. "The big buildings," cries Mother, "I can see them."

We almost enter the Gare du Nord. Then we perform a maneuver and set off again for . . . Reims, says the conductor.

"I can't see the big buildings any more," cries Mother again, "I want to see the big buildings." In fact, she can't take any more. She can no longer stay upright. She would like to sit down but can't because, in order to transport more people, they've installed three-story bunks; she has to stay lying down; lying down without moving for four days is exhausting.

Father speaks to the conductor: never mind about the orders, they must let the deportees off in Paris; from the capital, it will be easier to repatriate them to the various parts of France where they come from.

All this astonishes me, of course. How could I imagine, from far away, in my exile, that my sacked, ruined, plundered, martyred country would have to rebuild everything, start from scratch, recover its former glory.

Come on, we'll rebuild together!

The conductor allows himself to be persuaded, and the train starts off again in the direction of the Gare de l'Est, this time.

In the ambulance, we cross Paris at midnight. I observe everything and comment on everything out loud. I go from one window to another, and suddenly: "Mother, a shop called Francine, like me!" and the driver bursts out laughing.

The ambulance stops in front of a grand building, the Hotel Lutétia. Father explains that this big hotel, transformed into a welcome center for deportees, is going to put us up until we can return to our home.

The dark night, the badly lit streets.

We are taken to our room, on the first floor. Quiet corridors. The silent coming and going of smiling, friendly people.

Get into bed, sleep well. Tomorrow morning, the doctor will come and see you and give you any treatment you need.

It's already tomorrow, and I go to sleep, on 12 June 1945, and wish Father, who's thirty-eight years old today, a happy birthday.

So we left one another in 1939 on my joyful sixth birthday, and we were reunited in 1945 for my twelfth birthday, also joyful, of course, but how bittersweet.

The doctor comes into the room. Father leans against the wardrobe. I move back toward the window. Mother lies waiting. With the covers pulled up, you can see the collar of her khaki military shirt. Mother sketches a smile, grotesque, with her plucked chicken's head.

The doctor approaches, and taps her cheek:
"Don't worry, little fellow, we'll save you."

Then, we hear Father's deep voice:

"Doctor, that little fellow is my wife."

Grandmother, informed of our return, is due to arrive. She spent the end of the war hiding at our dear friend Clo's (who burnt our stars on the day we left in 1942), sleeping under the stairs, silent.

Father tells me about l'Abbé Ménardais, the chaplain for the little dancers at the Opera, a member of the Resistance who saved a great many Jews and Allied parachutists. It was in his network that Grandmother worked until the day he told her:
"Quickly, run to Clo's, they're going to arrest you."

I had got it into my head that Grandmother was going to arrive by bicycle, on her great friend the abbot's luggage rack, and I'm disappointed when I see her come out of the lift!

A shadow of her former self, my darling grandmother, but what a hug she gives me!

The doctor felt me, listened to my heart, turned me over, pawed me, examined me centimeter by centimeter.

I hear talk of a heart murmur, pitiful intestines, lack of calcium, serious edema of the legs, anemia. A long detailed list. I say I'm all right because I'm alive.

From our window, on the first floor, to the left of the entrance porch, I lean out and I look. In the center of the Boulevard Raspail, a wide pavement, on which big wooden billboards present the crowd with the names of the survivors, updated with each new arrival.

The people cluster anxiously around the posters. From time to time, someone gives a shout of joy and runs toward the hotel, another starts to tremble with emotion, unable to move, yet another faints.

When they see a deportee, they rush toward him: "Did you know so-and-so? Blonde, yes, tall, left such and such a prison on such and such a date. No? Ah . . ."

I see people who come back every day, once, twice, three times, and leave again, their backs bent, weary, exhausted. So many of them will come back like this, day after day, to consult the lists, until they're discontinued and the Hotel Lutétia closes.

Little Michel, on entering the hotel, overcome with panic, shouted:

  "My barrack-hut, my barrack-hut, I want my barrack-hut!"

Father has to go away, to take the message from Commandant de Rochcau to the Ministry. The others are waiting there . . .

He telephones the families of those who gave their numbers in Tröbitz.

Uncle Daniel, still in uniform, comes to get me. When I appear on the doorstep, the crowd falls silent, shocked. I hear a woman murmur "A child."

It's true, I am a child. An old child. A living child, and where I come from, Madame, there aren't many.

I even defy the German statistics, which give their deportees six months to live in the camps.

I total thirty-six!

No way of returning to our home. Our home no longer exists. This is the grand surprise of our return. Having completely stripped the apartment, the Germans had installed a collaborator and his family there.

It would be easy to evict him, but . . . during the Allies' landing, his house in the Cotentin was bombed. He was left with nothing and doesn't want to leave! During our imprisonment, he earned some money and wants to buy an apartment. In spite of that, he makes the most of the situation to get as much out of us as possible!

The loudspeaker outside that announces the names of the survivors keeps Mother awake. Once the first aid and the preliminary check-ups are over, we go to live with Grandmother.

Everyone is given a little package, very welcome because we have nothing left.

I'm given a dress (goodness, how beautiful it is!), some underwear, some socks, a sweater, a shirt, and some galoshes; some soap; and a parcel filled with sugar, little biscuits, sardines, and condensed milk; my repatriate's card, which serves as my identity card; and five thousand francs.

Each surviving French deportee starts out with these provisions.

I thank all the people from the Lutétia who, day and night, always present, always available, always "prepared," helped us return to life, then start a new life.

Jewish survivors, Christians, laymen, doctors, members of the Resistance, scouts of all three religions, devoted people from all walks of life, helpful, efficient, and good.

We live with Grandmother.

Decidedly, Mother is crazy, at least that is the verdict of the French doctors, whether members of our family or not. They want to put Mother in a convalescent home, and Father has to literally fight to explain and get them to understand this temporary madness brought on by the typhus. On the contrary, we must provide the gentlest and most comforting life possible, to speed up her renewed contact with the world.

Nothing shocks me any more, but when Mother talks to her "double," they all gasp.

Having seen her "double" pass by the window, Mother wants to follow her, and Father and I hold her down on the bed.

Through this same window, which looks onto the rue Cambon, I watch the goings-on between the American soldiers and the girls from the café-hotel. How do they manage to keep their hair up so high? And how do they manage to get so drunk? From time to time, the military police come to restore order.

When Mother calms down, Father and I go out. We get to know one another again, delighted.

And we discover that unknown world that is a free city.

Father gasps at the prices. "For the price of that cake, you know, before the war, you could have bought a whole meal." I don't believe him. He rages.

Never mind. On the way past Ladurée, in the rue Royale, our stomachs leap at the sight of choux pastries filled with cream! "Choux pastry!" says the salesgirl, "No, they're baked apples!"

Well, we'll eat them anyway.

Then, in ecstasy before a red leather handbag with a shoulder strap (all the rage!), "Father, please buy it for me, my first handbag!" "Leather!" says the salesgirl, "No, it's paper straw, plaited and painted!"

Well, we'll buy it anyway.

Really, could anyone, from over there, far away, could anyone have imagined that we would come back to find a country without flour, leather, trains, anything?

And completely penniless. The two little extravagances of the choux pastries and the handbag won't be repeated.

Father has no work. The money brought in by the first two books was taken by the Germans (and the books turned to pulp). The manuscript written in his prison camp was also destroyed by the Germans.

And it takes a good year to write a history book.

And then, he has to pay for treatment for himself, for his wife and daughter, and to get the apartment back.

In every family welcoming home a prisoner, he's the one everyone makes a fuss over. As for Father, he is one everyone forgot. In spite of his five years in prison, including one in a reprisals camp (which ruins your health!), there are more interesting cases. Poor Father. He rushes around every morning, writes in the afternoon, keeping half an eye on Mother, and produces articles for the newspapers at night to keep us in food, and which he publishes under other names.[34]

He has to find the money to pay the occupant of our apartment, who is asking for fifteen thousand francs to give it back to us!

Every Jewish family counts its missing. Nothing is intact. We are seen as strange animals, just think, all three sent away, all three returned.

My great-grandmother (I call her my "old grandmother" to distinguish her from the other "young" one) died at ninety years of age, unaware of the death of her two grandsons at less than twenty-five years of age, of Julien's two sons at the same age, and of Eugène's son, shot down.

After a few days, I'm sent to Nice, to Uncle and Granny's.

Uncle makes me work every day, to prepare for the new school year. It's true, I have to get started again.

Get started, find my feet, make a new place for myself in society, in a society that is nonetheless a little wary: after all, it's not as if I were a criminal!

Ah! My first contact with free people!

Who understands me, or rather, who wants to understand me?

There was the couple who wouldn't let their daughter come near me, in case I gave her my germs! But I've been washed, deloused, disinfected, brushed, scrubbed!

And those Germans, prisoners of war, digging the Albert 1st gardens in the sun, well fed, well dressed, and pitied by the passers-by. The poor things, having to work in the sun, to say that to me!

And the comments: "What, didn't they shave your head?" A little disappointed, no doubt.

And the endless questions:

"So what did you get up to, what did you children do to fill the time?"
　"Nothing . . ."
　"What do you mean, nothing, that's impossible."
　So, since I've had enough and I don't want to disappoint them, I make things up:
　"Well, they made us dig holes."
　"Holes, what for?"
　"To put stones in."
　"Stones? What good did that do?"
　"None."
　"None. But why none?"
　Oh leave me alone, leave me alone, I've forgotten everything.

How could I explain that it was precisely that, the horror for us children, doing nothing. Hanging around, day after day, our backs bent a little more every day, our stomachs tortured by dysentery, our flesh eaten by sores. Hanging around in the camp alley ways, breathing in the smell of burning men, counting the dead piled up to distract ourselves, comparing them (look, that one has a hairy chest, and that one has twisted feet), simply waiting for the end, the real end that sets you free, death.

"But did you really suffer a lot?" (A little skeptically.)

"Oh yes! A lot." (Then they seem satisfied.)

"They let you keep your clothes! So you were *kapos*!"

"Lucky for you they didn't tattoo your arm. The others have to wear a bracelet to hide it!"

"Don't eat so fast, it's bad for you, anyone would think you'd been starved!"

Mother is finally up and about, so she and Father come to join me in Nice. Ah! When I see them walking together, coming to meet me arm in arm, smiling; Father-Mother, my everything, my one-plus-one-makes-one.

But yes, I'm privileged! Even if we are sick, penniless, homeless, all three of us are here. I would like to write a song of happiness. This war leaves so many parents without children and children without parents.

And if some couples are reunited, how many can no longer be together again, be a family.

My parents' love, thank you for existing.

Mother sports a ravishing white hat, which frames her face well and hides her shaved head. The swelling in her neck is not going down very quickly.

But on the beach, in a sudden bout of annoyance, she pulls off her bathing cap. Everyone looks at her, and I quake with fear at the idea that she might be taken for one of those women shaved as a punishment, for "sleeping" with the enemy.

And I throw my towel over her head.

"But I can't stand always having my head covered any more!"

As for me, I try to puff up my still short hair to follow the fashion for high, high hairstyles.

Looking at myself in the (empty!) shop windows, my enthusiasm disappears. This silhouette, with its protruding stomach and heavy, blue-tinged legs, doesn't correspond to my twelve-year-old ideal.

I'm a little envious of these young girls who run after one another, so light on their feet, never getting out of breath, their skin smooth, their long hair in the wind.

The return to school seems the most difficult thing to me. I've been following my lessons, thanks to Uncle Charles's work, but I fail the entry exam for the first year at Racine, and my old school in the rue Jouffroy, with the same headmistress (what luck), takes me this year. I go straight into the second year at the Collège Octave Gréard, which takes me without an exam.

I am reunited with my young friends, and my two best friends, Christiane Moreau and Suzanne Bruneteau. You simply smile at me, without bothering me with these absurd questions. But I have trouble smiling back. Your little girls' concerns bore me. We no longer understand one another, for our chatter no longer coincides.

When you lose a member of your family, I shrug my shoulders at your grief. Come, come, how can you cry about someone dying!

You seem like babies, childish. Your games don't amuse me, your jokes tire me, your laughter annoys me, your secrets exasperate me. I can't follow you, our thoughts no longer run together, in parallel.

No, I am no longer of your world, I'm from a world apart, I'm from the world of the camps.

Back to Normality

Difficult and painful. Every deportee has had so many wonderful dreams in his camp, he's imagined so vividly the carefree, splendid, joyful life he would go back to, that the reality often destroys him.

Mother will not be going to a beauty clinic like she thought but will spend three years in terrible pain, with long months in bed, periods of calm thanks to the morphine, and finally an operation on her spinal column.

We get our apartment back by paying and borrowing, since the legal system is so slow that we cannot wait for a trial, even if we would win.

We find a few pieces of furniture that had been hidden (with such devotion), glad to receive the white wooden bed, stool, wardrobe, and table given by the State to each of the dispossessed.

Since France had been liberated a year before the camps, when Father returns, all the jobs are taken. Work in journalism and writing is given sparingly to those who choose those professions. Father, with the ball and chain that is my invalid Mother, will have to deal with the most pressing needs. On the one hand, working as a door-to-door salesman, carrying heavy suitcases. On the other, spending entire nights composing up to five articles for the same newspaper under five different pen names, and writing, finally writing, when I get home from school and can take his place as nursemaid.

I see Father, a few weeks after our return, almost crying at the shopwindow of a luxury delicatessen, exhausted by his sleepless nights and by Mother's suffering, because his wallet doesn't contain enough to buy one of these delicious treats for his wife. (At that time, writers had no social security.)

Both dreamed of having another child. It will be a son, we'll call him Bernard.
    Mother said: "My body needs a baby." But Bernard never came, because Mother was broken.

As for me, I do my schoolwork more or less well. Sensitive and sensitized to everything. In fifth year, my classmate Larroussinie, on learning that I am Jewish, shouts at me: "Filthy Jew, go back to your country!" Yes, Hitler sowed his seeds well.

I can no longer work at my lessons, and from that moment on, each day at school seems more painful to me.

No deportee ever truly returns from his camp, and every day I experience the living proof of that.

I like getting together with my ex–"boarding-house"

companions, as we say laughingly. We understand one an-other. And yet, how many dramas we have gone through since our return, witness this friend who loses her hus-band not long afterward, and then her twenty-five-year-old son, although she'd succeeded in bringing him back with her!

And another of our companions, who's good at every-thing, yet lives a completely stupid life, girls, nightclubs, brilliant studies, because he knows he is condemned, the doctors have told him. He dies at twenty-eight.

Many survivors are condemned.

Most have died since our return from the camps.

I will have to wait for the death of my grandmother, shortly after my eighteenth birthday, to finally realize what it means to lose someone dear to you, finally to be able to cry over someone's death.

Now

What remains of the camps for me?

Sometimes I wake with a start, prey to hallucinating nightmares.

I laugh at myself when I catch myself casting sideways glances at my neighbor's plate.

If I'm with a group of Jewish people, I always look for an escape route in case they came to arrest us. I prefer living in a building with two exits for that reason.

I'm afraid of dogs. I'm afraid of guns. I'm afraid of the dark.

Any Jewish massacre, whatever the nationality of the victims, totally devastates me, for I immediately see it as the sequel to the "final solution."

We are all hanged men and women saved by a broken rope.

Contact with Germans turns out to be difflcult. Not with young people. But whenever a German is of the "right" age, everything inside me curls up. In spite of myself, I imagine him in uniform, I see him in action, commanding, hitting, shouting.

The language, also, makes me ill at ease. The most beautiful *lied* or the most beautiful poem sounds only like barking to my ears.

I do not feel any hate toward Germany, if I did, I would be no better than my torturers.

In the end, maybe that's what it means to be Jewish: to possess a common experience of suffering and to practice the refusal of hatred.

Fifty years . . .

. . . Bergen-Belsen, I've just returned from there, for fifty years I've been waiting for this moment!

As I passed through the gate, something brought me up short: the birds . . . I could hear them singing everywhere . . . They ask me if there were no birds in the camps. I don't know. Maybe there were, but we didn't see them, because we saw and heard other very different things.

In Bergen, now, there are birds singing everywhere.

Oh! How splendid my camp looks!

I felt quite proud. It must be said that when I was eleven years old and spent a year here, it wasn't as splendid as this. Typhus raged and as the epidemic spread, the British troops had to burn everything, even the cremating oven.

So I walked and walked, almost with my hands stretched out in front of me like a blind woman, looking for landmarks, trying to find my barrack-hut, my infirmary, the place where they took the roll call.

Nothing. Everything is beautiful, everything is green, everything is peaceful, even the dark forest is lit by rays of sunshine. Here and there, there are large hillocks marked:

"Here 5,000 dead; here 2,000 dead; here number of dead unknown." But there are birds singing. I could quite happily have stretched out right there on the grass.

And then, in the museum, I saw the photos of the mass graves, the cart for transporting the bodies, people dying in the mud. Then I relaxed, I had found my childhood . . .

Fifty years . . .

To those of my aging camp guards who are still alive today, I say:

I have my Victory: I have my children and my grand-children."

Francine Christophe

In honor of those who taught me this song, written in times of freedom, and who sang it with me in times of oppression and are *all* dead.

Let's join our voices ere I part
I go to wander hill and dell
For life is sweet, the world so fair
So let us sing a last farewell

Chorus:
I roam the world with just my joy
And songs to keep my company
I sing of love, I sing of faith
The open road is calling me

I roam the towns, I roam the fields
Heart free from hate and pain
My pockets bare, I sing my songs
Which ring throughout the plain

And if I meet Death on the way
Among the poor he knows so well
He'll take me with him far away
And so I'll say a last farewell.

Chronology

1 SEPTEMBER 1939

Invasion of Poland by Nazi Germany.

General mobilization in France: on 26 August, Lieutenant Robert Christophe, called up, leaves his family on holiday in Deauville.

3 SEPTEMBER 1939

Great Britain and France declare war on the Third Reich.

AUTUMN 1939–

Drôle de guerre (Phony war, or funny kind of war).

MAY 1940

Francine and her mother live first at Cimiez, where Robert Christophe visits them on leave.

Then they return to Paris.

MAY–JUNE 1940

Campaign of France, debacle, and exodus.

Francine and her mother take refuge in La Baule.

Robert Christophe is taken prisoner.

AUGUST 1940

Francine celebrates her seventh birthday with her

mother and father, who is held by the Germans at the Grand Seminary in Laval.

Francine and her mother return to Paris.

SEPTEMBER 1940

Robert Christophe is transferred to an Oflag in Germany.

OCTOBER 1940

First anti-Semite legislation by Vichy.

Census of Jews by the French administration, on the request of the occupying German authorities.

MAY 1941

First mass arrests of Jews (foreigners).

Opening of Pithiviers and Beaune-la-Rolande internment camps.

20–25 AUGUST 1941

Second mass arrest of Parisian Jews: all men, French or foreign.

Opening of Drancy camp.

10 DECEMBER 1941

Jews residing in Paris cannot leave the city without special permission from the police commissioner.

12 DECEMBER 1941

Round up of the so-called "leading citizens" (heads of industry, intellectuals), almost all French.

It is no doubt within this context that the police come to arrest Robert Christophe.

7 JUNE 1942

Obligation for Jews in the occupied zone to wear the

yellow star, "from their sixth birthday onwards"; Francine is eight and a half.

16–17 JULY 1942

Round up at the Vélodrome d'Hiver in Paris.

For the first time, women and children are rounded up en masse.

20–22 JULY 1942

More than eight thousand internees from the Vélodrome d'Hiver are transferred to Beaune-la-Rolande and Pithiviers.

26 JULY 1942

Francine and her mother are arrested at La Rochefoucauld (Charente); they were trying to get to the South.

They are locked up in the function room at the Grain Exchange.

30 JULY 1942

Transferred to the prison in Angoulême.

3 AUGUST 1942

Transferred to an internment camp in Poitiers.

7 AUGUST 1942

Transferred to the camp in Drancy.

3, 5, AND 7 AUGUST 1942

In Beaune-la-Rolande and Pithiviers, two thousand mothers are separated from their children. They are then deported; the children will follow a few weeks later.

AUGUST 1942

Francine and her mother spend three weeks in the

camp at Drancy, which serves as a sorting and departure base for convoys of deported Jews. They meet children, separated from their deported mothers, who are en route to Auschwitz.

END AUGUST 1942

Francine and her mother are transferred for two or three weeks to Pithiviers. There they witness the departure of a convoy of deportees.

SEPTEMBER 1942

Francine and her mother are transferred to Beaune-la-Rolande. The camp is almost empty.

21 JUNE 1943

Return to Drancy.

MAY 1944

Francine and her mother are deported, with other wives and children of French prisoners of war.

7 MAY 1944

Arrival at Bergen-Belsen.

BEGINNING APRIL 1945

Departure from Bergen-Belsen. The S.S. transport the wives and children of French prisoners of war by train, including Francine and her mother, as well as some Dutch, Germans, Greeks, etc.

15 APRIL 1945

Liberation of Bergen-Belsen by the British troops.

23 APRIL 1945

The S.S. abandon the train.

Liberation of the deportees by the Red Army at Tröbitz (80 km south of Berlin).

2 MAY 1945

Robert Christophe's Oflag is liberated by the British troops.

6 JUNE 1945

After a month's search, Robert Christophe is reunited with his wife and child in Tröbitz.

Notes

1. Translator's note: In Britain, it was called "The phoney war."
2. Alfred Weill, my uncle, and Albert Christophe, my cousin, would be shot in 1943, with a group of their comrades from the Resistance. One of their comrades, shot at the same time and left for dead by the Germans, managed to drag himself to a farm and tell his tale. There is a monument in Maves (Loir-et-Cher) to their memory.
3. A specialist in venereal and skin diseases, he was the first to set up a medical service reserved for a certain type of lady. He was a doctor at Saint-Louis and Saint Lazare, where he treated Madame Caillaux after her imprisonment. His fascinating memoirs would be worthy of a book, which he refused to write.
4. Translator's note: Head of the collaborating Vichy government, who was condemned to death after the war.
5. World War I hero.
6. Her blind elderly mother would go to the church at six o'clock every day to pray for us, right until the end of the war!
7. Ex–Prime Minister of France (1936).
8. Translator's note: The author is referring to Joseph Darnand, the founder of the French "Milice."
9. Mother is head of the barrack-hut.
10. The gift was a small flowering plant.

11. There are sixty signatures on this letter delivered by Mademoiselle Rolland, a social services assistant with the Red Cross, who bought the gift outside, and added "With my affectionate best wishes." Sixty women who hope: I can count only six survivors!

12. After the war, Uncle Charles still shook with rage when recounting this anecdote.

13. His wife Madeleine, who was to die prematurely, managed to keep his pharmacy in the rue Duphot, passing herself off as an Aryan and a collaborator, and obtained much information from her German clients. The day of the Liberation, Grandmother, who knew about her activities as a member of the Resistance because she belonged to the same network, ran to her and said "Quickly, put on your tricolor armband, people in the *quartier* think you're a real collaborator, and they'll shave your head!"

14. His name was not on the list, but he did not want to leave his friend.

15. As told by the concierge and Madame Paul, the grocer.

16. They escaped from their train. One of them lost a leg in the attempt.

17. A well-known French prison in Lyons.

18. We had been granted permission to write a letter to France! Mother therefore wrote to a friend of Grandmother's, Mme. Quéval, so that Grandmother would not be discovered. She then gave our Bergen-Belsen address to Father.

19. This letter was kept by my grandmother.

20. Grandmother sent it to her in a parcel at Beaune-la-Rolande.

21. Doctor Alalouf was decorated by Queen Wilhelmina of Holland after the Liberation.

22. Mother, in spite of the strict night curfew, went to the hospital anyway, accompanied by a German barrack chief, because she wanted to see the doctor about Madame S . . .

23. This was the same typhus epidemic that killed Anne Frank and her sister Margot, also imprisoned at Bergen-Belsen.

24. Imagine my shock on discovering a photo of the Baur family, fifty years later, on page 385 of the Memorial for Jewish children by S. Klarsfeld!

25. Many managed in spite of everything to get qualifications and jobs, honoring the country which they wished at all cost to consider as their own, but these countries are not always loyal . . .

26. It was to become the Israeli hymn.

27. At least what remains of them. These diamond cutters, refusing to work for the Germans (who needed their professional skills) were separated from their children. Some of the men were sent to other camps.

28. This fear so marked me that, many years later, its memory still overwhelms me.

29. Buttoned on the side and with fur caps.

30. In truth, we changed even before we ate. Throw away these revolting rags, hurry, hurry, hurry.

31. Fifty years later, a man with a handsome smiling face would say to me "I'm Maurice Zylberstein, the one who shouted to you, 'Francine, your father's here.' "

32. We repeat this to one another every year on 6 June.

33. It was only later that Leipzig would pass under Russian control.

34. During his imprisonment, he exchanged his parcels for letter forms, so that he could write to everyone to get us set free. (See *Une Famille dans la Guerre*, published by L'Harmattan.)